METTLE

Foreword by Jayesh Ranjan, IAS, Principal Secretary to Government of Telangana, Departments of I&C and ITE&C

METTLE

THE STUFF WE'RE MADE OF

INSIGHTS INTO HYDERABAD'S TOP INDUSTRIES AND HOMEGROWN ENTREPRENEURS

POORVI KALLURI PAWAR

www.whitefalconpublishing.com

Mettle - the stuff we're made of
Poorvi Kalluri Pawar

www.whitefalconpublishing.com

All rights reserved
First Edition, 2022
© Poorvi Kalluri Pawar, 2022
Cover design by White Falcon Publishing, 2022
Cover image source freepik.com

No part of this publication may be reproduced, or stored in a retrieval system, or transmitted in any form by means of electronic, mechanical, photocopying or otherwise, without prior written permission from the author.

The contents of this book have been certified and timestamped on the Gnosis blockchain as a permanent proof of existence. Scan the QR code or visit the URL given on the back cover to verify the blockchain certification for this book.

The views expressed in this work are solely those of the author and do not reflect the views of the publisher, and the publisher hereby disclaims any responsibility for them.

Requests for permission should be addressed to
poorvi.pawar@gmail.com

ISBN - 978-1-63640-766-1

Dedication

To every curious person who has ever picked up a book to expand their knowledge.

Foreword

Jayesh Ranjan IAS

Principal Secretary to Government of Telangana,

Industries & Commerce (I&C) Department, & Information Technology, Electronics and Communications (ITE&C) Department

Mahatma Gandhi used to say that India lives in its villages. Today, this statement may still be true technically, as villages hold more of our population as compared to cities, but the reality is that cities have become the primary engines of growth. While different metropolitan cities in India have their own significance and heft, no other city exemplifies the spirit of aspiration and rapid transformation as Hyderabad does.

I first came to Hyderabad about 30 years ago, after getting selected in the IAS and getting allotted to the then combined cadre of Andhra Pradesh state. I was born and brought up in Lucknow, and for many years, found nothing greatly dissimilar between Lucknow and Hyderabad - both languid capital cities of two large states. But if we assess what heights Hyderabad has reached today, as compared to what it was just about 3 decades ago, or even 2 decades ago, or even a decade ago, it will appear like an unbelievable science fiction story. Hyderabad has today become an economic powerhouse supporting industries and services as diverse as IT, life sciences, aerospace, tourism and hospitality, and healthcare, to name the most prominent ones. Particularly in the last 8 years, since it has become the capital of the new state of Telangana, the economic buoyancy and social vibrancy of the city has been enhanced manifold.

One good fortune that has come Hyderabad's way is that successive governments, regardless of dispensation, have supported the creation of infrastructure required for the expanding needs of the city. The enterprising private sector has also kept pace, and brought high quality amenities to the citizens. It is no surprise therefore, that Hyderabad gets ranked as the best Indian city for quality of living on multiple indices.

Behind every significant transformation in Hyderabad's journey, there are key people who have played a crucial role in leading by example and creating something visionary that impacts the entire sector of their activity. We have been very fortunate that such spirited individuals were able to carry the entire ecosystem along, so that whatever they initiated was supported and then replicated by many others. I am personally very fortunate to have known and worked with many of the pioneers profiled in this book. Today, we have a very thriving IT and industrial manufacturing sector. But the fact is that the foundations of making Hyderabad an attractive destination were laid decades ago by these pioneers. The same holds true for other industries covered in the book like healthcare, construction, food and agri processing, etc.

One priority area of the current Telangana government of which I am a part, is to promote innovation and entrepreneurship. While every entrepreneur's journey is unique, there are surely common lessons to be drawn from the paths they have traversed. 'Mettle' is a fascinating attempt by Poorvi to capture the essence of their personality, their work ethic, their strategies, their vision and goals, all of which stand behind their visible success. This book is also a chronicle of all the key moments that have made Hyderabad pivot to the next level, in its exciting growth story. I found going through the book to be very educative and motivating. I am sure that other readers too will feel the same.

Contents

Introduction 1

PART - I

Editor's Note on Healthcare and Pharmaceutical Industry 8

Interviews

    Krishna Prasad Chigurupati 10

    Dr Gullapalli Nageswara Rao 18

    Dr Ramesh Kancharla 26

Industry insights: From Malaria to COVID, the city's progression into a global pharma and healthcare hub 33

PART - II

Editor's Note on Food and Agri processing Industry 44

Interview

    Dodla Sunil Reddy 46

Industry insights:

    Hyderabad's dairy diaries - Fostering South India's white revolution 54

    The Poultry Industry - All eggs in Hyderabad's basket 59

    Food and Agri-processing 65

PART - III

Editor's Note on Infrastructure Construction and Building Materials Industry	70

Interviews

AAV Ranga Raju	72
K Ravi	80
Jalandhar Reddy	88
Industry insights: Infrastructure Construction and Building materials Fundamentally strong	96

PART - IV

Editor's Note on Aerospace and Defence Industry	104

Interview

Dr Amar Nath Gupta	106
Industry insights: Aerospace and Defence industry: Soaring high	113

PART - V

Editor's Note on The Tourism Industry	122
A Tourist Hub	124

PART - VI

Editor's Note on the Services Sector	136

Interviews

J A Chowdary	140
Vanitha Datla	152
Industry insights: Hyderabad to Cyberabad: The tech revolution that put Hyderabad on the world map	161
Disclaimer	177
Editor's Acknowledgements	181

Introduction

Today, every brand, leader, organisation, industry and even country has their own story. Storytelling is a well-calibrated art. Stories have a deeper reach and stay longer in the minds of people. Experiences and emotions, when wrapped around facts, have a distinct ability to capture the imagination of the reader.

Every reader feels a unique emotion when he reads words. The challenging task of the writer or editor lies in evoking such emotions and putting together those meaningful messages. The ultimate reward is knowing that the words made a difference to the reader and played their role beautifully.

The leaders interviewed for this book possess an immense wealth of knowledge gained through decades of experience. Through their stories, we shall try to understand the guiding principles behind their success.

There is a beautiful Sanskrit maxim on knowledge-sharing so relevant to this book.

"Apoorvah kopi koshoyam vidyate tav Bharati Vyayato vruddhim aayaati kshyam aayaati sanchayaat."

When translated, it means: 'A treasure trove of knowledge increases when shared, and decreases when stored within'.

I have always been intrigued by life questions. What is our purpose? How does one develop deep convictions? How is it that only some people achieve great heights of success, glory and altruism while the rest merely exist until they perish? And so on. Throughout my professional career, I raised these questions in conversations with friends, colleagues, and business leaders with whom I came in contact. I loved the perspectives these conversations brought about. I admired the intense focus of people who did things with unwavering faith and often pride. This, perhaps, laid the foundation for this book.

My quest in the interviews with Hyderabad's top business leaders has been to understand the characteristics, traits and beliefs of these leaders and bring them out in a simple conversational tone.

The questions cut across the various aspects of a personality to get into the mindset and persona behind the business leader. What is the philosophy of business founders? Who influenced their thought processes as they grew up or set about their mission? What are their passions and hobbies? I put together twenty-five questions that draw out a brief life story of these leaders. The outcome, in my opinion, is wonderful mini-biographies, quick to read and understand the stuff these leaders are made of. Through their stories, they share knowledge and experience, which can educate, inspire and motivate students, professionals, entrepreneurs, homemakers, and anyone willing to learn.

I chose business leaders from Hyderabad, where the founding families are still at the helm of the business, proud and sincere in upholding the mission and vision behind their business. The attempt was to get a good cross-section of the city's leaders from different industry verticals. There were a few more that I would have liked to interview but could not due to time and availability constraints. My conversations with them yielded wonderful insights and, at times, unravelled less known facts about them. It gave a perspective on their life until now and also their expectations for the future. I realised that their passion for their business was so profound that their personal and business goals seamlessly flowed into each other.

Innovation, adaptability and resilience are cornerstones of growing businesses, which are amply displayed by the leaders I spoke with.

The leaders themselves are a mix of first-generation and second-generation entrepreneurs. Several times, they talked about complex business challenges faced by them and how they were overcome. In every instance, beliefs and core philosophy played a big role in how they responded to such challenges, and I discovered some very interesting techniques used by these leaders. I expect you will also find these helpful in your personal and professional life.

The backdrop of the stage of the evolution of the business sector played a key role in enabling the growth of businesses in Hyderabad. As I spoke with the entrepreneurs, it was interesting to note how they faced business challenges such as being too early to the market or being a first mover at the right time; of how policy regulation in their industry played a significant role in impeding or aiding their growth. This prompted me to delve deeper and research the evolution of the prominent industry sectors in Hyderabad. How did industry originate and sustain in the city? What were the key drivers to growing scale? Which are the leading companies in the city? The research yielded several valuable nuggets of information regarding each industry, which I have documented in this book.

I hope you find the interviews and industry insights an engaging read. I express my deepest and most sincere gratitude to everyone who has indulged me in my journey of bringing out 'Mettle'. I am immensely happy that these amazing business leaders aligned with my purpose of knowledge-sharing and freely told me their stories. I enjoyed gathering details about each of the industries and uncovering lesser-known facts about the city's rich and interesting heritage and evolution.

And as for the interviews, to me, these deeply personal human stories are always the most honest way to inspire others.

Insights into Hyderabad's business landscape

Hyderabad is perhaps well known as an IT capital and, more recently, India's vaccine hub and pharma city. While it is definitely all of these, it is much more than the IT and Pharma industries. The city hosts several other prominent industries and harbours thousands of MSMEs doing specialized work, employing lakhs of people. This book chronicles their evolution, focusing on homegrown entrepreneurs, policy makers, events and facts that have shaped them and brought them where they are today.

Some information was obtained through dialogue and research, while some through interviews of people in the city who were witnesses to this journey. It is fascinating to understand the macro scenario of the nation and the state at the time each of the industries started and the challenges and policies that enabled their evolution. The first movers, the game changers and how critical mass came to be are important in each industry.

The book attempts to provide narratives and lesser-known facts, as opposed to statistical information on industry size and other such details. Needless to say, with the present business environment in a post-pandemic world, all industries continue to evolve amid disruptive technology and new consumer behaviour.

About Hyderabad

Hyderabad is my proud home and the backdrop of this book. I have watched it evolve over about two and a half decades now. The newer parts of the city sprung up and rapidly developed during this time, while the older parts retain their pace, heritage and culture. The transition of cultures, preferences and lifestyles is palpable as you navigate the different parts of the city, whether on foot, by public transport or in cars. Hyderabad is an accommodating city that lets you pick a pace and lifestyle that suits you.

The city has a mix of Hindu and Muslim cultures and traditions. Telugu, Urdu and Hindi are widely spoken in Hyderabad, making it easy for Indians from across the nation to communicate in the city. The Nizams were connoisseurs of literature, art and music and left the city with a rich heritage of architecture, monuments, museums and culture. You also find a range of cuisines, a melting pot of cultures and pleasant tropical weather year-round to entice visitors, temporary workers and NRIs in equal measure.

The economy blossomed over the decades, and there has been an influx of people from various Indian states, who are all happy to live and even settle down in Hyderabad. The infrastructure, employment opportunities, educational institutions of repute, global presence, and logistically well-connected city make it one of the best places to work and live.

Hyderabad is strategically located in South-Central India, with excellent connectivity by air and rail. Within the city, public transport options consist of APSRTC (State) buses, local suburban trains (the Multi-Modal Transport System or MMTS), metro rail, cabs and auto rickshaws. The MMTS and Metro rail are wonderful low-cost transport options with tremendous connectivity across the city, helping the expanding city and its populace cope with road congestion. The MMTS has an annual ridership of about eight million passengers, while the recently inaugurated Metro rail has close to five million. The Nehru Outer Ring Road allows travellers to avoid city traffic and drive on spacious, multi-lane highways akin to driving on Interstate highways in the United States. The Rajiv Gandhi international airport is a world-class greenfield airport operated in the public-private partnership model. It is one of the most awarded airports in the world and handles about 21 million passengers and 1,48,000 tons of cargo annually. The airport has massive expansion plans with an aim to develop 'Hyderabad airport city' into an integrated ecosystem with industry-specific zones for warehousing, logistics and cargo management.

In terms of economy, Hyderabad is driven by both manufacturing and knowledge sectors. While the early roots of Hyderabad began as a major trading centre, the 1930s and 1940s saw the development of manufacturing industries, with an import of technology from the western world. The pharmaceutical and electronics industries blossomed during the 1970s and 1980s. On the manufacturing front, auto components, precision engineering and building materials saw an increasing number of mid and large companies establishing a base in the city. The late 1990s and 2000 saw explosive growth in the service sector, with the information technology revolution leading it. The city has since diversified into a broader spectrum of services such as biotech, financial services, insurance and several ancillary industries like real estate and retail.

The history of capital markets in Hyderabad with respect to public issues is as old as 1930 when VST Industries went public. Later, in 1941, the Hyderabad Stock Exchange (HSE) was established. After achieving many milestones, the HSE was disbanded by SEBI in 2007. During these years, numerous local companies from the pharma, chemicals, electronics, information technology and construction industries went public.

As of December 31, 2021, among the top 10 listed pharma companies based on market capitalisation, four companies are from Hyderabad. Among the top 100 companies listed on the BSE from across all sectors, only three are from Hyderabad, and all are from the pharma sector, i.e. Divi's Labs, Dr Reddy's Laboratories and Gland Pharma. Today there are over 200 listed companies in Hyderabad, of which about 50 are actively traded. In the last few years, several Hyderabad-based companies came out with their IPOs, to take part in the boom in primary markets. The ₹6,480-crore IPO of Gland Pharma was one of the largest pharma sector IPO in recent times. KIMS Hospital is the second hospital IPO from Hyderabad after Apollo, and it raised ₹2,144 crores upon its listing in June 2021. Among other recently successful IPOs from the city are MTAR, Vijaya Diagnostics, Dodla Dairy, Rainbow Hospitals and MedPlus.

The ten business leaders profiled in the book have chosen Hyderabad as the headquarters for their operations. This city has hundreds of successful entrepreneurs and is home to many vibrant and thriving business industries. The digital revolution, the rising prominence of the pharmaceutical industry amid a global pandemic, and a new wave of startups across the spectrum, combined with collaboration with top-notch educational and research institutions, make for ample opportunities to study and work in the city.

PART - I

Healthcare and pharmaceutical industry

Editor's Note on Healthcare and Pharmaceutical Industry

Having worked in a multinational pharmaceutical company for more than eight years, my routine work involved keeping up to date on the pharmaceutical arena. And I was always fascinated by how much Hyderabad has achieved in this field. With a chronology of great achievements ranging from crucial research for tackling malaria that took shape here in the 1890s to the current development of an indigenous COVID vaccine for India by Bharat Biotech, the city has indeed nurtured a high share of entrepreneurs in this field. The field of science has found a significant place in the city with its multiple applications in human life, from agriculture to medicines, research to genetics, and nutrition to biologicals.

Hyderabad has already entrenched itself as a major hub for innovation and collaboration in the pharma space. Prestigious research institutes such as NIPER, CCMB and NIN provide the crucible for fostering talent and industry collaboration to the ambitious enterprises thriving in the city. The state government has always ensured full support in the form of incentives, infrastructure and land, with plans for special parks being customised for sub-segments of the pharma industry—a medical devices park, Pharma city, and genome valley 2.0. Apart from policy and infrastructure support, there is immense focus on innovation and incubation of start-ups in this field.

Contributions in the field of medicine are far and wide and involve several professions. Dedicated and hard-working doctors, nurses and staff dispense diagnostics, medicines and treatment to a burgeoning populace. Major clinic and hospital networks find a place in Hyderabad,

Mettle

attracting several doctors, nurses and medical practitioners to the city. Therefore, it is not surprising that the city is becoming a medical tourism hub. Manufacture of bulk drugs, formulation medicines, marketing, clinical research and contract research has created employment opportunities for lakhs of individuals.

As Hyderabad continues to evolve in the new post-COVID era, it is my attempt to recount how the city has emerged as a global pharma hub. The entrepreneurs who dared to dream and envisioned the present scenario need due recognition. Profiled herein are three such dynamic entrepreneurs who have made a mark in the city. They continue to work tirelessly and relentlessly to serve the public through their work. Their humility and passion made a deep impression on my mind, and I cherish my conversations with them. The people I interviewed, their journeys, traits and characteristics, and a chronicle of the industry is presented in this section of the book.

Krishna Prasad Chigurupati

Founder and Managing Director
Granules India Ltd.
www.granulesindia.com

Krishna *Prasad Chigurupati is a first-generation entrepreneur from Guntur. As a young man, he was not keen on following in his doctor father's footsteps; instead eager to experiment with business. After a string of failed entrepreneurial ventures during his early years, he founded Granules India Ltd. in 1991. Starting as a paracetamol API manufacturer, Granules has since grown into a multi-faceted pharmaceutical company with a global presence. Apart from running the business, Krishna Prasad and his wife have a claim to fame in the Guinness Book of World records for running seven marathons on seven continents. The duo also successfully converted their passion for wine into a business and ran a boutique wine label KRSMA and have a vineyard in Hampi.*

Established In
1991

Revenue for FY 20-21
323.7 crore

Number of employees
3398

Units/Locations
8 manufacturing facilities

Markets present
75 countries

Expertise
Manufacture of APIs, PFIs and Finished Dosages

Highlights
World's largest PFI facility

Filings
51 ANDA filings

INTERVIEW

We started our virtual meeting about five minutes late, and Mr Krishna Prasad Chigurupati was quick to apologise for the delay. We exchanged pleasantries and realised that we would have preferred an in-person interview and decided to postpone such a meeting to another day. Thus started off our one-and-half-hour interview where we reflected, laughed and discussed so many aspects of life, in general, and his life, in particular. It was so easy to be awed by the amazing achievements of an ordinary man who decided to stand out from the crowd. His easy demeanour, strong convictions and list of tremendous personal achievements made for instant fandom and reinforced in me the motivation and joy of doing what I set out to do.

So what is it that makes you spring out of bed each morning?

Progress on my new ideas. It enthuses me in the mornings. I think about these things when I am running or working out in the mornings. Interestingly, in my sleep, I also get new ideas or changes in ideas and remember everything when I wake up. I think about these things as soon as I wake up.

What do you believe is the purpose of your life, personally?

My purpose is to distinguish myself from everyone else in whatever I do. Whether it is business, fitness or other personal goals, I ensure that I do things that make me stand out. I spend time nurturing the things I do, and I get amazing results from them. This makes me feel purposeful and fulfilled.

At what age do you think you identified this, and what were your motivating factors?

During my first year, while doing my B.Sc. in Guntur, I realised that I did not want to study; rather, I wanted to do something on my own. I had very good exposure in terms of knowing the world around me, although academics did not interest me per se. I think by this time, I had decided that I wanted to go out there and build something from scratch on my own. I forayed into business young, and through many years of ups and downs, I now have something I built and am proud of.

Who or what has been the greatest influence in your life? A person, a book, a saying or a transformational moment you'd like to describe?

I can't think of any single person or book that transformed or shaped my life. I just followed my instincts and, most of the time followed the least trodden path.

They say the morning habits set a person's day up for success and productivity. What's the morning routine like before you get to work?

I ponder on the events of the past few days and review progress on short and long-term goals. I plan the day, and after this, I get down to two hours of different workouts and yoga.

What was the last most interesting book you read and why?

I read a lot of fiction by authors such as Tom Clancy, Frederik Forsyth, Arthur Hailey, etc., during my college days, but I don't read much anymore. I don't do academic or other reading either. Instead, I have other hobbies.

Which book do you think everyone must read and why?

The one book I respect a lot is the *Mahabharatha*. It gives knowledge about life. The characters, the plot and the depth of the story contain a lot of learning in it. I think everyone must read it.

What hobbies do you pursue currently, and how often do you find time for them?

Running is a hobby I picked up at 50. My wife and I ran seven half-marathons on the seven continents and set up a Guinness record for it! Wine making is a hobby, and we bought a vineyard at Hampi Hills and manufactured high-quality wines. Cooking is a hobby, and

I enjoy making grand and delectable dishes with various meats. Photography was a childhood hobby, and I have recently picked up bird photography. I find time to pursue my hobbies on most weekends.

What do you think is the biggest lesson you learnt in 2020, the year of COVID?

Never take anything for granted and to see opportunity in everything, even in disasters. We never stopped our production work during the pandemic, but we used the time to take care of our people, stand by them, do our bit for society and be thankful every day for everything we had. During the pandemic, all the employees and I spent time eating the same food together every day in the open. I used the time to motivate people to do business. There are a few unanswered questions, such as why there is so much suffering, why it impacted some parts of the world more than others, and so on. However, gratitude and opportunity in crisis are two big takeaways from the pandemic for me.

What's your favourite quote of all time?

This is borrowed from Ratan Tata "I don't believe in taking the right decisions. I take decisions and then make them right." There is never a perfect opportunity.

What do you tell yourself when you face insurmountable challenges? Typically, things where you need to make tough decisions?

Generally, I do not look at anything as insurmountable. I am always positive and continue to work in my normal way, tweaking decisions on the go but never giving up. I could overcome most of the challenges, but once I realised that I would not be able to overcome some, I was quick to drop them.

Do you feel stressed and overwhelmed? What do you do to cope with stress?

I cook! Cooking with a glass of wine by the side is a huge stress buster. I make big feasts, steak, seafood, lobster sushi, burgers, lamb etc. It really helps me relax, and my friends and family get to enjoy the meals.

What is the single piece of advice you would like to give your peers?

Follow the 3 P's–Passion, Patience and Persistence.

Have you thought about how you'd spend your time after retirement?

Retirement from the business may happen, but retirement from life won't happen! I have many things on my bucket list, and I like being physically and mentally active!

How do you measure yourself? Do you have quantitative or qualitative goals that you track and measure yourself against?

I don't measure myself too much and take things as they come. However, I do set short-term goals for myself. Every year they may be different- sometimes top-line, sometimes bottom-line, sometimes a new market, or new products and processes. Sometimes the goals extend beyond the original period they were set to. Apart from this, I have always achieved well in my hobbies, such as running and wine-making.

What are a couple of words your family would use to describe you?

That I am foolishly passionate :) Once I set my eyes on something, I do everything possible to achieve it! That's what my family would say about me.

What is the one piece of advice you'd give your children?

To do well in academics, acquire discipline and work for someone else. They also need to learn how to sell their skills. I want them to have the ability to stand on their own feet anytime in life. Everyone can earn money, but earning respect is harder. I want them to understand that and earn both, if possible.

How do you approach difficult conversations and conflicts? Could you share what has worked for you?

I avoid and procrastinate when there are conflicts. I am a conflict-averse person. Eventually, I tread the middle path. I think it is a weakness, and I am ok with it.

What was the last vocational or professional course you took, and did it help you?

About 12-15 years ago, I did a course at the Indian School of Business. It was a very productive workshop, with a lot of examples and case studies, which I could apply to my projects at that time. I don't really do continuous education, however.

Do you have a connection with your hometown/place of birth/ community?

I am from Guntur, Andhra Pradesh. I left my hometown when I was about 18 or 19 years old. My mother still lives there, but she visits me more often than I visit her there. I don't have any deep friendships in Guntur, so I'd say I don't have much of a deep connection with the place anymore.

What is the best form of giving back to the society you have experienced and would advocate for others?

I believe in doing something for education and health. At Granules, we have a CSR initiative where we bring bright high school students from rural areas, put them in good hostel facilities, and train them in various life skills. We then give them training at our manufacturing facilities and employ them with pay. After three months of training, we enrol them into an online program for B.Sc. We tied up with a few universities, who come and take a couple of classes on campus. Once these students graduate, we set them free. They can continue to work for us or to work for others. We don't bind them at all. Our goal is to help them get a degree and a skill so they can stand on their feet. This program is very dear to me. When some of these kids flourish and come back to tell us how well they are doing, it really warms my heart.

What is the legacy you wish to leave behind?

That, I am a person who lived life on his terms.

How do you define happiness? How often do you find yourself in this state?

I am happy with what I am doing and what life has given me. I don't like to complain. I generally don't get angry easily either. In the tensest of situations also, I did not experience sadness. I see opportunity in everything. I look for a silver lining in every cloud. I'd say I am mostly happy. Sometimes I may be annoyed, but I am never really unhappy.

Any lesser-known facts about you that surprise people?

That, I am not a graduate.

What does spirituality mean to you, and how does it influence your approach to life?

I don't have any opinion on spirituality. I like to be good to people and not harm them. At this point, I don't think about spirituality, but maybe at some point in the future, it may matter to me.

What role has education played in preparing you for the role you are now performing

My thinking and my analytical things helped me a lot in life. Basic principles of chemistry, physics etc., have helped me in my work. Knowing about the world around me through my books, travel, television etc., also helped me a lot. Since I did not complete my graduation, I'd say formal education in terms of degrees has had less of an impact on my overall life and business.

Do you believe in discipline and routines, or are you a spontaneous person?

I'm mostly a spontaneous person. I don't let the discipline aspect curtail me with my spontaneous ideas. It is difficult to be regimented when running a business; one needs to be flexible. However, once the business reaches a level of scale, it is difficult to be spontaneous, and I've found the right balance of discipline and spontaneity. When it comes to my personal hobbies, such as running, workouts etc., I am very disciplined.

Dr Gullapalli Nageswara Rao

Founder-Chair
LV Prasad Eye Institute
www.lvpei.org

Padmashri Dr Gullapalli Nageswara Rao is a leading opthalmologist, Chairman of the Academia Ophthalmologica Internationalis and the founder of the L.V.Prasad Eye Institute. Dr Rao completed basic medical education at Guntur and did his postgraduate residency training at the All India Institute of Medical Sciences (AIIMS), New Delhi. Renowned globally in the field of Opthalmology, he has received numerous awards, recognitions and accolades for his work spanning about five decades. Dr Rao has five honorary doctorates from Australia, India and the UK. He founded LV Prasad Eye Institute with a mission to provide affordable eye care for the Indian masses. While the dream started with providing 50% of the services free, the vision has broadened in scope to include everyone looking for eye care. Having grown up in a village, Dr Rao has deep empathy for the lives of people in rural India. He uses his training and global exposure to execute his mission to bring equitable eye care to the underserved populations in developing countries across the world.

Established In	Outpatients	Units/Locations
1987	**17.55** million	**234** eye care centres in 4 states

Community initiatives – reach	Highlights	Eye surgeries
12.76 million	Equitable and quality eye care to all sections of society	**1.79** million

Expertise

Clinical Services, Education, Research, Vision Rehabilitation, Rural and Community Eye Health, Eye Banking, Advocacy and Policy Planning, Capacity Building, Innovation and Product Development.

INTERVIEW

The screen lit up with Dr Nageswara Rao's bright personality, in his signature 'bow-tie and crisp shirt' look, and I briefly introduced myself. His down-to-earth nature and warmth struck me as soon as we started the interview. Dr Rao is a Padmashri awardee, a very eminent and dedicated ophthalmologist, but more than all of his accomplishments, he is a wonderful human being! In the short time that we spoke, he made everything in his life feel easy and normal, including his narrative of his journey. He answered all questions to the point with immense clarity of thought. He chuckled and laughed while talking about himself. He spoke with passion about the role of discipline, rigour and doing one's job well in life. His retirement goals involve further giving back to society in the field he has chosen. He spoke of the many people whose biographies inspired and motivated him, which is just what I hope reading this mini-biography does to many others.

So what is it that makes you spring out of bed each morning?

I am an animal of habits, and that is what makes me get out of bed every day. Sometimes I wake up earlier, which usually means I have to meet a deadline.

What do you believe is the purpose of your life, personally?

The purpose of my life is to be a good human being and help people as much as I can in what I do.

At what age do you think you identified this, and what were your motivating factors?

I can't point to a time when I realised this; I think I have been incrementally influenced throughout my life.

Who or what has been the greatest influence in your life? A person, a book, a saying or a transformational moment you'd like to describe?

There have been so many great influences on my life. Speaking of the days post medical college, my mentor in Post Graduate

Ophthalmology, Professor L.P. Agarwal, inspired me with his discipline, focus, rigour and broad vision for life. Most of my mentors taught me that incredible rigour in whatever you do, meticulous attention to detail and regularity in completing work are important traits. I've also been influenced and shaped by many books, such as the biographies of Mahatma Gandhi and Nelson Mandela. I have also been motivated by the biographies of several medical leaders.

They say the morning habits set a person's day up for success and productivity. What's the morning routine like before you get to work?

The first thing I need in the morning is a cup of strong coffee. I would call myself a coffee addict. I usually walk for about 45 minutes five times a week. I then clear all my overnight emails and messages before I get to the office.

What was the last interesting book you read and why?

I was recently gifted the book 'Space Life Matter', The Coming of the age of Indian Science by Hari Pulakkat. It contains lots of interesting stories of many unsung heroes of science. The people who made progress in science possible in India. It is not only interesting but inspiring as well.

Which book do you think everyone must read and why?

A book that I think everyone must read is 'The Checklist Manifesto' How to Get Things Right by Atul Gawande. It is a fantastic book that clearly points out that when we adopt rigorous practices, the quality of outcomes is much higher. There are numerous case studies and use cases in hospitals and other walks of life that have been cited in the book. A checklist is also important for airline pilots. To sum up, the book shows how anybody who practices checklists in everyday work can accomplish much more. I also highly recommend another book by Atul Gawande called 'Being Mortal: Medicine and What matters in the end'. It is about the last years of people's lives and what they expect at that time. It is about the struggle to care for them at such times. The book has several life lessons in it.

What hobbies do you pursue currently, and how often do you find time for them?

My biggest hobby is sleeping. I also like to watch some television to relax. I also love reading. I used to read a lot earlier than I do now. I like simple fiction and biographies. I read over weekends, holidays, flights, and a little before going to bed every night.

What do you think is the biggest lesson you learnt in 2020, the year of COVID?

The world was totally unprepared for the pandemic. Despite all the signals of an impending pandemic, we were insensitive and oblivious of what would happen. I now worry that we may have a similar situation with climate change. I am afraid that we are going to pay a very heavy price in the not-so-distant future. At one point, I used to be jealous of my next generation, but now I am worried for them because of the side effects of climate change, which will impact them heavily in the next two-three decades.

What's your favourite quote of all time?

"Those who bloom late bloom in full." I came across many instances where this was proven to be correct.

What do you tell yourself when you face insurmountable challenges? Typically, things where you need to make tough decisions?

I get all the information needed to make my decisions. Once I do that, I make the decision, accept the outcomes and move on.

Do you feel stressed and overwhelmed? What do you do to cope with stress?

I am lucky to have never really felt stressed about anything.

What is the single piece of advice you would like to give your peers?

Choose what you really like to do in life and do it well. Do not waver from your chosen destination. One can get anything in life if they want it badly enough.

Have you thought about how you'd spend your time after retirement?

I am working on a few areas over the next few years.

1) To make eye health more accessible and efficient in rural India. 2) To facilitate community development in areas where we work. 3) To get involved in global eye health programs in West Africa. We are currently running a program in Liberia that can be scaled for West Africa if it does well. 4) To participate in international discussions on eye health. 5) To do some writing

How do you measure yourself? Do you have quantitative or qualitative goals that you track and measure yourself against?

I don't measure myself; I just keep doing what I do. I think others should measure me. My job is only to do my best.

What are a couple of words your family would use to describe you?

Perhaps I am a workaholic and boring :)

What is the one piece of advice you'd give your children?

I would give everyone the same advice-peers, children and everyone. Whatever you do, do it properly. You are serving someone with it. Make sure no one is hurt by your actions.

How do you approach difficult conversations and conflicts? Could you share what has worked for you?

I approach them by being as transparent and as frank as possible. Whenever there is difficult news to convey, it is better conveyed swiftly. E.g. Poor performance feedback. I prefer to have direct and open discussions. I don't give up on people easily. I think everyone has inherent capabilities, and we must find a way to bring them out.

What was the last vocational or professional course you took, and did it help you?

For 45 years, I have been learning by observing, studying and interacting with professionals, institutions and organisations. Leaders in various fields, including non-medical fields, have helped me and taught me so much in life. It has been a very long since I took a professional or vocational course. While I have taught courses, I haven't taken up anything myself. However, I have learned through every informal channel available.

Do you have a connection with your hometown/place of birth/community?

I have a close connection with the village where I grew up, Edupugallu, near Vijayawada. I used to visit it once every two months before COVID. I still have friends from every stage of my life, including my childhood in my village.

One of the greatest forms of wealth that I accumulated is my exposure and my ability to keep in touch with people from all stages of my life. I am as comfortable in my village as at a luxury hotel in New York City. I have travelled far and wide and can appreciate every place, situation and conversation I have had.

What is the best form of giving back to the society you have experienced and would advocate for others?

Society invests in every individual. If you do whatever you are doing well, that in itself is giving back to society. In the medical profession, we have a unique and unusual combination of doing well and doing good. If you want to do both, you can. Sometimes the medical community is accused of veering toward doing well versus doing good. However, there is always a choice for us. Doing good is very important.

What is the legacy you wish to leave behind?

My philosophy is to do my best in life, and when it is time to walk away or walk out, to do it gracefully. I am not too concerned about whether it leaves a legacy or not.

How do you define happiness? How often do you find yourself in this state?

I am happy most of the time. A child whose sight is returned makes me happy. A child with cancer whose life we could save makes me happy.

We run various training programs for youth from underprivileged families. Watching them grow and flourish makes me happy. When everything in the family is going well, I am happy. I believe I have been fortunate to have never really suffered. If one is not greedy, the chances of being unhappy are limited.

Any lesser-known facts about you that surprise people?

That I never won any gold medals. I was always in the middle third of my class. Also that I grew up in a small village. Growing up in a village made me stronger and truly Indian.

What does spirituality mean to you, and how does it influence your approach to life?

I do not understand the word spirituality. Some say I am spiritual because of what I do and how I do it. However, I consciously do nothing to say that I am spiritual, nor do I claim to know it.

What role has education played in preparing you for the role you are now performing?

Education has obviously played a very significant role in what I do. The cumulative impact of my education has made me what I am today. I owe a lot to all my teachers and mentors, right from my village school to all the informal teachers of life.

Do you believe in discipline and routines, or are you a spontaneous person?

I strongly believe that discipline is very important to achieve something. A combination of brilliance and discipline helps people to accomplish the most. Brilliance alone will not help people get ahead in life. Discipline is an absolute necessity.

Dr Ramesh Kancharla

Chairman & Managing Director
Rainbow Hospitals
www.rainbowhospitals.in

Dr Ramesh Kancharla is a first-generation entrepreneur hailing from the Nellore district. As one among seven siblings, he followed his brother's advice and decided to earn a degree and do something meaningful in life. Dr Ramesh got his MBBS degree from SV college in Tirupati and went on to get an MD in Paediatrics from Kasturba Medical College. He had a long stint as a paediatrician in the UK and was enamoured by the fantastic infrastructure of paediatric hospitals in the country. In 1999, he returned to India and, together with his friends, decided to establish a chain of hospitals focused on children. Thus was, born Rainbow Hospitals–which now has plans to expand its presence in cities across India, with a plan to enter Tier 2 and 3 cities in the upcoming years. Dr Ramesh is moving purposefully towards his dream of providing child-focused hospitals across the spectrum–from birthing, diagnostics and treatment of diseases to complex surgeries such as transplants.

Established In	Revenue for FY 2020-21	Number of employees
1999	**650** crore	**3995**

Locations	Number of beds	Expertise
14 Units, 6 Cities pan-India	**1500**	Children's and Obstetrics hospital

Highlights
India's largest pure-play pediatric hospitals

INTERVIEW

I arrived three minutes late for interviewing Dr Ramesh Kancharla, feeling bad about being late yet not wanting to appear nervous. I was shown in immediately, and his PR team asked me a question or two, stated a preference to record the interview, and within minutes we were set to start. We introduced each other briefly, and I thanked him for opening a children's hospital, having taken my kids there on various occasions. In fact, both from a women's and children's hospital perspective, I and several of my peers have been to Rainbow Hospital on multiple occasions. Dr Ramesh said he would prefer a free-flowing conversation to a Q&A format, which feels rigid. I smiled and agreed happily. And the conversation flowed, up to almost two hours, a genuine and honest story of the humble beginnings, of a first-generation entrepreneur from Chiramana, near Nellore district. A story of two decades, with bumpy beginnings and subsequent viability, of impressive growth and bold future plans. Behind this was the vision of a simple man—to make children's speciality treatments a reality for India, at affordable costs and built purely on trust.

So what is it that makes you spring out of bed each morning?

Building a strong team behind Rainbow Hospital makes me proud and happy. We are well reputed and financially viable. For the first 10 years, we addressed India's need for children's hospitals. For the next 10 years, we built all the specialities for children that existed for adult patients. Now my main job is mentoring, building other teams, and expanding and growing the group business. This motivates me every day.

What do you believe is the purpose of your life, personally?

Together with my colleagues, I founded the Rainbow Children's Hospital because I found that India did not have the type of hospital facilities for children that I had seen in the UK and US. Complicated surgeries like transplants were done at adult hospitals, and multi-bed exclusive children's hospitals were non-existent in India. By building a multi-city children's speciality hospital chain that is a living and breathing organisation, I think I have fulfilled my purpose.

At what age do you think you identified this, and what were the motivating factors?

My initial ambitions were limited to being a very good paediatrician. When I returned to India from the UK in 1999 and surveyed the existing facilities, I decided to set up this hospital with a few colleagues and found my calling.

Who or what has been the greatest influence in your life? A person, a book, a saying or a transformational moment you'd like to describe?

My parents and my older brother Ravindranath. I am one of seven siblings and was raised in a small village near Nellore. My father was the village head, so he used to be away a lot, helping people, solving their problems, resolving conflicts and so on. My mother had to raise and manage seven of us, and she had excellent managerial skills. Our family was originally affluent, but when we were growing up, times were a little tough. I think because of this upbringing, I have the ability to adapt to any conditions and live happily. My brother Ravindranath became a doctor and motivated me to also take up a serious profession. Of the seven children, two of us are now entrepreneurs, both running two hospitals. So, to sum up, my father, brother and mother have been the biggest influences on me.

There is one transformational moment in my journey of Rainbow that I must share. After the initial years of not finding success with the hospital, I managed to get an audience with the then chairman of the Andhra Bank. I made bold but honest statements, criticised the bureaucracy of the bank, and put forth my list of requirements that would help us keep going. It was our last chance to try and survive as a hospital. Within 24 hours, he did his best, giving me almost everything I requested for. This was a turning point for our hospital, and I am still grateful for it. Once we survived the initial years, we grew both in reputation and financially, and there has been no looking back since.

What was the last most interesting book you read and why?

I used to read Telugu fiction and novels during my student days. I haven't really read since then. I am a good listener; I prefer to observe and listen to people.

Which book do you think everyone must read and why?

I don't have any recommendations as such.

What hobbies do you pursue currently, and how often do you find time for them?

I love listening to music and exploring luxurious spas. I like relaxing in lounge bars and eating at good restaurants. This is mostly what I do in my spare time.

What do you think is the biggest lesson you learnt in 2020, the year of COVID?

Clearly, the world was hit by something no one anticipated or could handle. The healthcare systems world over were exposed. The world was thrown into panic. However, in India, a few things turned out as a blessing in disguise. Perhaps some of our bad habits, responsible for our good immunity, saved us. India and Africa had fewer deaths than the developed countries in Wave 1. I felt there were more benefits; for example, parents started bringing children in only for vaccinations. Since everyone was indoors, there was less incidence of disease and people did not panic and bring children to hospitals for every little thing. Many pregnant women were able to carry their babies to term. Statistics may not be available, but I suspect neonatal, and maternal mortality rates should have improved in 2020.

What's your favourite quote of all time?

I don't have any quote as such, but I believe in adding value to people around me.

Do you feel stressed and overwhelmed? What do you do to cope with stress?

Yes, there is stress sometimes, but I know how to switch it off. Sometimes there are internal problems that leave me thinking intensely for days. But these are all phases, and they get over. In the end, most days I don't think much when I go back home. For this very reason, I feel not marrying into the same profession is very helpful because I can leave work at the office and completely switch off when I get home.

What is the single piece of advice you would like to give your peers?

Help patients build trust in you, as trust keeps healthcare costs in the country low.

Have you thought about how you'd spend your time after retirement?

I don't think anyone should retire unless they are a vegetable. Retirement can be from frontline responsibility from strategy, but one can still be involved at the board level. If one is merely occupying a seat, one must retire.

What are a couple of words your family would use to describe you?

Soft and sensitive.

What is the one piece of advice you'd give your children?

That humility is very important, especially in the lower strata of society. When doing rounds, I make sure I give a proper audience to those in the general ward who are afraid of speaking up. I tell my son to do the same and to keep going back to the general ward until everyone there has had their questions answered.

What was the last vocational or professional course you took, and did it help you?

I don't really do any courses as such. After my academics, I have learned everything else on the job.

What is the best form of giving back to the society you have experienced and would advocate for others?

Building a trustworthy chain of hospitals, aspiring for India's ability to conduct complex transplants for children in children's hospitals -this, I believe, is my contribution to society.

What is the legacy you wish to leave behind?

My soul will be happy to see the organisation grow beyond me, making it more efficient and taking it to the next level.

How do you define happiness? How often do you find yourself in this state?

Happiness is having free time and spending it on things I like. Good friends and music make me happy.

Any lesser-known facts about you that surprise people?

I am a very honest and transparent person, so I don't think there are any lesser-known facts about me.

What does spirituality mean to you, and how does it influence your approach to life?

I believe in a higher power, a God, but not in idol worship and temples. I think spirituality means reflecting on things like equanimity and how to move forward in life.

What role has education played in preparing you for the role you are now performing?

Education laid the foundation and is hugely responsible for getting me to where I am today. Sometimes I miss the fact that I am not seeing patients and practising medicine; however, knowing that I have built a corporate chain of hospitals compensates for that lack, in part.

Do you believe in discipline and routines, or are you a spontaneous person?

My mother was a strict disciplinarian, and we were brought up with tough love. So I'd have to say I believe in discipline.

From Malaria to COVID

The city's progression into a global pharma and healthcare hub

Introduction

Medicines are an inevitable part of human life, consumed to cure or alleviate people's health conditions. The importance of the pharmaceutical industry has tremendously increased after the COVID pandemic took the world by storm in 2020. While the discovery, manufacture and distribution of vaccines have taken centre stage, vaccines are just one part of the larger pharmaceutical industry.

Primarily, the pharma industry consists of manufacturing, R&D and marketing units.

The manufacturing units consist of API/bulk drug manufacturing, formulation, and contract manufacturing for larger companies or institutions.

The R&D units consist of new chemical entity research, formulation research, or contracted research for larger companies or institutions, including clinical trial research.

The marketing units are especially dedicated to marketing services. They trade in drugs manufactured by other companies.

Hyderabad rankings in India

Hyderabad now ranks first in manufacturing bulk drugs (also known as Active Pharma Ingredients or APIs) in the country and third in manufacturing formulations. It is also the Vaccine Hub of India and is growing in the clinical trial sub-sector of pharma. Hyderabad is also taking the lead in contract development and manufacturing organisations (CDMO), with a few established players and several smaller firms.

Notable names of homegrown large pharmaceutical companies are Dr Reddy's Labs, Aurobindo Pharma, Divi Labs, Natco Pharma, Hetero Drugs, Gland Pharma, and Neuland Labs, Granules Ltd. and Laurus Labs. Bharat Biotech, Biological E, Shantha Biotechnics (now Sanofi), Indian Immunologicals and Globion Bio are notable names in the vaccine space. Vimta Labs, Jupiter Biosciences, Quintiles and Sipra are prominent in the clinical trial sector. Avra Laboratories, Aragen Life Sciences (formerly GVK Bio), Sai Life Sciences and Laurus Synthesis are some of the well-known players in the CDMO space. It is indeed a matter of pride for one city to have so many famous and established players in an industry that is a niche, R&D based, and highly technical.

The pharma industry contributes in a major way to the economy, healthcare and affordability of treatments for Indians, apart from being a major exporter and service provider to international giants and important to the exchequer of the state and central government.

How it all started

The pharma industry journey of the city truly started in the 1950s, with Biological E Ltd. entering the medical sciences field to do commercial business.

In the 1960s, the city started becoming more established as a pharma hub mainly due to two reasons.

The first was the creation of the Indian Drugs and Pharmaceuticals Ltd. (IDPL) by the Govt. of India in 1961, as the largest public sector manufacturer of drugs, with an aim to make the country less reliant on imports for life-saving drugs. It was the vision of Late Pt. Jawaharlal Nehru to setting up an organisation with twin objectives of self-sufficiency in life-saving drugs and doing it affordably. The Hyderabad plant was started in 1967 in the Balanagar area and manufactured about 47 bulk synthetic drugs. However, the manufacture of bulk drugs and formulations at IDPL has stopped, and only an effluent treatment plant is in operation.

DID YOU KNOW?

Did you know that the path-breaking discovery of mosquitoes as a carrier of the malarial parasite happened in Hyderabad? In 1893, Sir Ronald Ross was a British surgeon stationed as a medical officer in Secunderabad Cantonment. During his stay in the city, he conducted research on malaria, confirming that the malarial parasite is carried in the body of mosquitoes. The Nobel prize for his work was conferred on him in 1902. This important discovery was made at a building in Begumpet. The building where this research was conducted was anointed as the Ronald Ross Institute of Parasitology, and several donations, grants and efforts went into preserving this as a heritage building for some decades, although it is devoid of activity now.

The second key factor that enabled pharma growth in Hyderabad was the evolution of Jeedimetla as an area of development of ancillary units for IDPL in 1977. Jeedimetla has many process equipment manufacturing companies and is much larger in terms of physical area than other well-known industrial areas such as Patancheru, Sanath

Nagar, Katedan etc. Jeedimetla had a lot of ancillary companies in not just pharma but other industries such as plastic, engineering, precision components, etc.

These two factors and the availability of infrastructure led to the attraction of a talented pool of technical people to the industry. The city is home to some top research scientific institutes such as the National Institute of Pharmaceutical Education and Research(NIPER), the Indian Institute of Chemical Technology (IICT), Centre for Cellular and Molecular Biology (CCMB), along with a plethora of private colleges offering pharma related courses, which makes the availability of talent pool even easier.

The next set of entrepreneurs in the city was truly inspired by Dr Anji Reddy. After a stint at the National Chemical Laboratory, Dr Anji Reddy joined IDPL. Following his entrepreneurial instincts, he left IDPL in 1974 and established two companies - Uniloids in 1976 and Standard Organics Ltd in 1980, experimenting with manufacturing bulk drugs independently. He also founded Cheminor Drugs, which Murali Divi of Divi Labs fame helped grow in the initial years. In 1984, he established Dr Reddy's Labs in Hyderabad, which catapulted him to fame, putting Hyderabad on the global map of pharma. Dr Anji Reddy is credited with making Hyderabad the bulk drug capital of India and realising his grand vision of low-cost drugs in India. When Dr Anji Reddy entered the bulk drugs industry, there were barely any entrepreneurs in that space, and the industrial policies were very restrictive. Using his skills of scientific knowledge, grooming talent and building processes, he built his business step by step. He disrupted the industry by bringing bulk drug prices down by almost 50% early on. He then took the bold step of making formulations to bring the overall cost of drugs down for the end consumer, the Indian patient of fewer means. He then added research, the essential ingredient in a complete pharma organisation that helps discover new medicines. The meticulous combination of quality, processes, technology and capital contributed to the success and fame of Dr Reddy's Labs.

Dr Anji Reddy is also renowned for his generosity in supporting, nurturing and encouraging other major pharma companies in

Hyderabad. Murali Divi of Divi Labs, P.V. Ramprasad Reddy of Aurobindo Pharma, B. Pardhasaradhi Reddi of Hetero Drugs, MSN Reddy of MSN Laboratories, Venkat Reddy of Lee Pharma, Chigurupati Krishnaprasad of Granules India and Raghavendra Rao of Orchid Pharma were all nurtured by him. These domestic pharma companies have played a key role in bringing affordable generic drugs to India and their own R&D units, leading to the discovery of several new molecules.

The first private Pharma entrant

The earliest private venture in the pharma space in the city was Biological Products Pvt. Ltd. (now Biological E Ltd.), founded in 1953 by Dr D.V.K. Raju and Mr G.A.N. Raju. The company originally started manufacturing anti-coagulants and pioneered Heparin production in India. With an aim to bring affordable vaccines to India, it was the first private company to enter the vaccine business in 1962. During the 1960s and 1970s, the company started large-scale production of sera and vaccines, developed formulations in cough and digestive enzymes, commenced manufacture of anti-tetanus serum, and launched anti-TB drugs, TT and DTP vaccines. By the early 2000s, the company focused on producing low-cost vaccines and launched its flagship vaccine product, Pentavalent, in 2008. Today, Biological E Ltd. has four core businesses: vaccines, generic injectables, formulations and synthetic biology. It has leading partnerships with major governments, not-for-profit organisations and research institutes across the world, notable ones being the WHO, UNICEF and Pan American Health Organization. The company supplies vaccines to over 100 countries across the world and made revenues of close to INR 500 crore in the year 2020.

A massive growth phase

Starting from the 1980s, the next three decades saw about 2,500 pharma companies of varying sizes coming up, with some of the most notable ones aforementioned. With a homegrown industry and easy availability of talent, the city started attracting a number of multinational companies such as the Swiss pharma giant Novartis, American firm Mylan Laboratories (now part of Viatris) and others.

Hyderabad also has many pure-play CDMO companies. Avra Laboratories, founded by the ex-Director of IICT, Dr A.V. Rama Rao, in 1995, was one of the pioneers in this space. Many larger pharma companies, homegrown and multinationals, now have CDMO as a standalone business segment. Additionally, there are a growing number of smaller players and startups coming up in Hyderabad due to the large availability of experienced professionals and student talent. Several factors shape the CDMO landscape. Multinational pharma companies have all jumped on the bandwagon of life sciences and research, and outsourcing makes it easier for them to achieve their goals. The pandemic exacerbated the importance of strategic outsourcing in a global scenario and emphasized that mitigating the risk of over-dependence on a single country such as China is important.

Today, Hyderabad is the proud home of numerous established pharmaceutical companies, as well as cutting-edge research and development. It is the development and operations hub for several multinationals and is also witnessing several startups in the healthcare technology space. Slowly and diligently, she made her way to become one of the most famous pharmaceutical hubs in the world.

Future forward: Pharma City, Genome Valley 2.0 and Medical Devices Park

The Government of Telangana is planning to establish a dedicated infrastructure space of about 19,000 acres catering to the entire value chain of the pharma industry, known as the Hyderabad Pharma City. This is proposed to be an integrated facility, considering factors such as smart infrastructure and sustainability, incorporating things like effluent treatment, solid waste management and ensuring minimum pollution. This Pharma City is coming up in the Mucherla area near Hyderabad. Apart from this, Genome Valley 2.0 and a Medical Devices Park are also planned, with an aim to catapult Hyderabad as the pharma destination of choice.

Buzzing with Biotech

The biotechnology industry emerged as an important sub-sector of pharma, although it has applications as wide as human and animal healthcare, agriculture, environment and processing industry, thus extending beyond what traditional 'pharma' addresses. India's biotechnology industry got a major boost with the establishment of the Department of Biotechnology (DBT) in 1986. Today, India is among the leading 12 destination nations for biotechnology worldwide, which the DBT aims to take to the top five. Apart from furthering the education, research and translation ecosystem of the country, the DBT is credited with enabling startups through the Biotechnology Industry Research Assistance Council (BIRAC). The BIRAC supports intellectual property rights and the commercialisation of inventions to help SMEs and researchers bring out better products with good applications and at lower costs.

Hyderabad is well placed in the biotech space. Its story began with early players such as Shantha Biotechnics and Transgene Biotek. Transgene Biotek was founded in 1991 and started off as a manufacturer of diagnostic kits before becoming a focused, full-fledged biotech research company. Founded in 1993, Shantha Biotech made India's first indigenous recombinant hepatitis B vaccine and launched it in 1997. The company supplies vaccines to leading organisations such as UNICEF and PAHO. In 2006, the company was acquired by Sanofi.

In 1999, the city got a dedicated, pollution-free, state-of-the-art space in the form of Genome Valley, a public-private partnership between the state government, Bharath Biotech, Shapoorji Pallonji Group and ICICI Bank. Located at Shameerpet, this is India's leading R&D cluster with world-class facilities, multi-tenanted wet laboratories and incubation facilities. The companies here are engaged in a wide range of specialities such as agri-biotech, clinical research management, biopharma, vaccine manufacturing, regulatory and testing. Within 20 years, Genome Valley became home to more than 200 organisations and 50 multinational R&D labs and research centres. Several international partnerships and tie-ups have aided the development of Genome Valley. With a planned Genome Valley 2.0, and more interest in establishing or increasing base in the city, the contributions from Hyderabad in the field of biotechnology can only be expected to increase.

Healthcare hub and medical tourism

Hyderabad is becoming a major healthcare hub and an attractive destination for medical tourism. The city houses about 50 government hospitals and over 150 private hospitals, apart from some 4000+ clinics and nursing homes and 500+ diagnostic centres. Notable multi-speciality private hospitals such as Apollo Hospitals, Yashoda Hospitals, KIMS group, Care Hospitals (now part of Evercare Group), Rainbow Hospitals (paediatric) and AIG are well renowned in the country. There are a couple of more recent entrants in the hospital space who are struggling to keep their heads above water, as it is not that easy to attract and retain good doctors and get patients. There seems to be higher potential in speciality care, cancer hospitals and other areas of specialised research these days.

Medical tourism is the provision of 'cost-effective' private medical care in collaboration with the tourism industry for patients needing surgical and other forms of specialised treatment. In India, this process is being facilitated by the corporate sector involved in medical care as well as the tourism industry—both private and public. India provides a good base for medical tourism due to the large availability of doctors, technology and infrastructure in the form of good super speciality hospitals, at a fraction of the cost in the western world.

The many advantages that Hyderabad offers are commendable. Accredited facilities and top-notch infrastructure, availability of qualified physicians, surgeons and hospital support staff, fluency in English speech, and significant cost savings when compared to western regions such as North America and the UK. Some hospitals also offer a private room, a translator, a private chef and dedicated staff, factors which are attractive and affordable when compared to similar services in the West. Lastly, the city's connectivity in terms of airlines and airports is an added advantage to those looking to make a choice.

The Center for Cellular and Molecular Biology (CCMB)

The Council of Scientific and Industrial Research (CSIR), Delhi, established 44 research institutions across the country. Notable among these were the IICT, CCMB and National Geophysical Research Institute (NGRI) in Hyderabad, all established in the Uppal area.

In 1987, the Hyderabad campus of CCMB was inaugurated under the aegis of Dr P.M. Bhargava, amid a 'galaxy of scientists' including six Nobel Laureates, one of them being Dr Francis Crick, famed for decoding the Double Helix structure of DNA along with Dr Watson in the 1950s. The centre was established with the objectives of conducting high-quality basic research and training in modern inter-disciplinary areas of biology. Dr Bhargava was passionate about Hyderabad and played a significant role in turning Hyderabad into a 'Science City'. The institute is known for some of its path-breaking work, such as the increased use of DNA fingerprinting. Another breakthrough research was the study of Aryan and Dravidian races, conducted in collaboration with Harvard and MIT. This study established that the current Indian population is a mix of ancient North Indian and South Indian and that the long-perpetrated belief that Aryans and Dravidians signify ancestry of north and south Indians is a myth.

The CCMB is also credited with supporting the incubation of Shantha Biotech, the growth of Sun Pharma and the Sanghi industries group in Hyderabad. The organisation has since expanded with a laboratory for the conservation of endangered species in Attapur and a medical biotechnology complex in Uppal.

Hyderabad is also home to the Centre for DNA Fingerprinting and Diagnostics (CDFD), an autonomous organization funded by the Department of Biotechnology (DBT), Ministry of Science and Technology, Government of India. In 2019, CCMB and CDFD signed a Memorandum of Understanding to enable, through scientific research, a better way of diagnosis and treatment of genetic disorders, thus continuing to make big strides in biotechnology and genetics.

Mettle

DID YOU KNOW?

Padmashri Dr B. Somaraju, eminent cardiologist and founder of the city's CARE hospital, collaborated with Missile Man of India, former President Bharat Ratna and Padma Bhushan Dr.A.P.J. Abdul Kalam to develop the 'Kalam-Raju' stent for coronary heart disease. This life-saving stent was introduced in the 1990s and brought down the price of stents by more than 50% for India.

Dr Kalam, who led the Defence Research and Development Organisation, was moved by the accounts of poor patients suffering from cardiac problems at the state-run Nizam's Institute of Medical Sciences (NIMS), where Dr Soma Raju, a friend of the former President, was the director.

Dr Kalam and Dr Raju used state-of-the-art defence technology to design the stent. The specially designed coil and a metal-based stent were priced at INR 7,000/-, way cheaper than the commonly used stent, which is available for INR 30,000/-. The stents, which started being manufactured by some ancillary units of the defence sector, became popular with patients in NIMS, many of whom were implanted with these stents.

PART - II

Food and Agri processing Industry

Editor's Note on Food and Agri processing Industry

So much is taken for granted in our daily lives. For a majority of the middle class and upwardly mobile families, food comes with a wide variety of choices these days. The food on our plate has a journey that begins at an agricultural, dairy or meat farm. I was pleasantly surprised to discover the depth and breadth of the food and agri processing industry in Hyderabad. The city impresses with research institutes such as the NG Acharya Ranga Agricultural University, ICRISAT and National Institute of Nutrition (NIN), which contribute immensely in their respective fields. I also discovered that the city covers a broad spectrum of the food and agri processing industry. Biscuit manufacturing for indigenous consumption and exports, a dairy industry with milk and value-added products, a poultry industry with eggs and chicken, meat production and processing- every segment has a notable presence in the city. It is a source of livelihood, employment and enterprise for lakhs of people. Numerous nationally known brands in the food processing industry, such as the Bambino group, Priya pickles, Dukes biscuits and 24 Mantra, have their origins in Hyderabad.

While traditional manufacturing facilities and processing centres have established themselves firmly, there is a new interest in home-growing and homemade food. Organic farming, organic snacks and homemade foods, pickles, confectioneries and baked goods have entered our lives. A number of micro-entrepreneurs began thriving in this unorganised space and continue to delight customers with their exemplary range of product and service offerings. At the same time, there is also an immense appetite for bistros, delis, bakeries,

Mettle

restaurants and food joints of all shapes, sizes and specialities. Chutneys, Paradise and Pista House are now world-famous chains that belong to Hyderabad.

The section that follows details three sub-segments of the agri and food processing industry, dairy, poultry and meats, and packaged foods in Hyderabad. From titbits to stories behind the early years, you will find all the exciting information in this section.

Profiled in this section is a business leader from the dairy industry. The last two and a half decades witnessed explosive growth in the dairy space, with packaged milk and value-added products finding a place in almost every kitchen and refrigerator. Time constraints and double-income families paved the way for quick access to products traditionally made at home. Everything from buttermilk, paneer and ghee is available in conveniently sized and packaged forms. Chilling centres, dairy farm practices and farm feed have developed and evolved, creating an ecosystem for efficient production of milk and milk products. Large private dairy players bring sustainable income, support and stability to the lives of dairy farmers. All of these factors contributed to the growth of the industry thus far and will continue to propel it forward. Read on to know more about one of the most successful dairy entrepreneurs in South India.

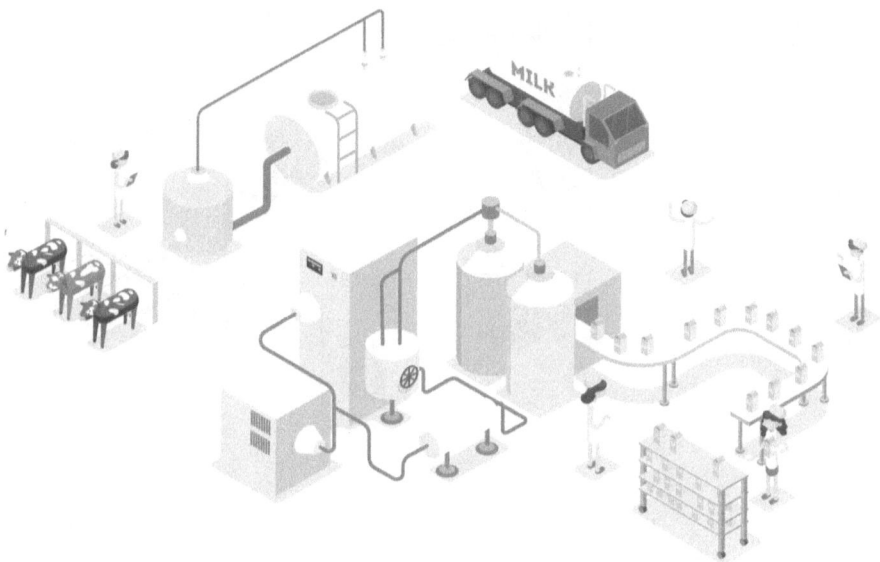

Dodla Sunil Reddy

Managing Director
Dodla Dairy Ltd.
www.dodladairy.com

Dodla Sunil Reddy founded Dodla dairy in 1995 in Chennai. He is a second-generation entrepreneur. However, dairy was a new field for him as his family was in the infrastructure business. Sunil did industrial engineering at Manipal and decided rather early on in life that he would be an entrepreneur. He is happy to have found his calling in the dairy industry. Today Dodla is a leading dairy company in South India, supplying milk and value-added products through distributors and retail dairy parlours. The procurement of milk is centred around five states, and the products are available in 11 states across the country. The company has also invested in dairy feed, research and dairy farming.

Established In **1995**	Revenue for FY 20-21 **1944** crores	Number of employees **2551**
Processing units **14** in 4 states	Sales offices **42**	Number of farmers **1.3** lakhs
Installed capacity **20** LLPD	Dodla retail parlours **546**	Distribution agents **3100+**

INTERVIEW

I arrived at the office of Dodla Dairy bright, early and very enthusiastic as it was the first interview I had secured for my book. As I waited for Mr Sunil, I got some time with the CEO, Mr B.V.K. Reddy, who entertained and informed me about many facts regarding Dr Varghese Kurien and the White Revolution.

As I walked to his office, I couldn't help but admire the buffalo and cow-themed art adorning the walls, surfaces and alcoves of the management floor. Stunning metal art and paintings depicted their sincere acknowledgement of how the humble animal is central to their business.

And then I met the man himself. An extremely affable leader with a big smile and instant warmth. He comes across as very friendly and down-to-earth, giving credit to so many people in his life for the success he has now achieved. He was gracious to allow the interview to be conducted in two parts and patiently participated in the conversations with me.

Mr Sunil made an important observation 'ethics pass through generations'. He was raised to believe strongly in giving back. While loyalty as a concept has evolved from the 1960s until now, and people are inclined in future to live more for themselves and sacrifice less for others, ethics will be rooted in people throughout their families and will continue to survive.

So what is it that makes you spring out of bed each morning?

Life has been good to me, both personally and professionally. So I look forward to each day. I am mentally in a good place, happy and therefore I think every day has to be celebrated!

What do you believe is the purpose of your life, personally?

My purpose is to leave a mark, a legacy that I created. I am fortunate to belong to a family that has made its mark in Nellore. For five generations, our family has been known in our hometown, and I want to ensure that I am able to contribute further to this.

At what age do you think you identified this, and what were the motivating factors?

I guess I was in my 11th or 12th class at school when I realised I wanted to do something that was my own and that I could leave behind for the next generations.

Who or what has been the greatest influence in your life? A person, a book, a saying or a transformational moment you'd like to describe?

It has been different people at different stages in life. I think from a family perspective, my grandfather and father both influenced me. My grandfather's brother did a lot for the community, and my grandfather was his man Friday. He moved the family from a village to a town, whereas my dad moved us from a town to a city in terms of exposure. There have been several others in my early career who influenced me.

They say the morning habits set a person's day up for success and productivity. What's the morning routine like before you get to work?

During most of my youth, I was not a morning person. I always stayed up late into the night while developing my business. Luckily, for the last 15 years or so, I have had a friend who takes me for a walk at 05:30 am. So now, my morning routine involves physical exercise for about an hour every day.

What was the last most interesting book you read and why?

'How the Mighty Fall: And Why Some Companies Never Give In' by James.C.Collins and James.M.Collins because it shows you how small and stupid things can destroy everything that has been built.

Which book do you think everyone must read and why?

Hotel by Arthur Hailey-because I like the story and what it conveys. There is an old guy who is high on ethics and builds up wealth but is not arrogant about it. Nobody knows that he has built the wealth, and he saves the day when no one expects him to. That character has stayed with me throughout.

There is one more thing I read that is very useful to me. Harvard Business Review, short articles that give insights about businesses, the world today and how to tackle challenges. These articles serve as a quick reference and help those looking to solve business problems or to keep up with the latest trends.

What hobbies do you pursue currently, and how often do you find time for them?

Reading has been my biggest hobby, and I was a voracious reader in my younger days. Other than that, I like to grow things, like, fruits, for example. I collect seeds and sow them and watch the plants grow into trees. I am learning golf now and play whenever I can. Walking every morning has been a steady hobby for the past 15 years.

What do you think is the biggest lesson you learnt in 2020, the year of COVID?

I think COVID showed us that fear can change everything. Society was gripped with fear of contracting the virus, making everyone fearful of one another! The other lesson learned is that things can actually keep running without you, and you may not be as important as you thought yourself to be.

What's your favourite quote of all time?

My favourite is not a quote but the first story in the Art of War by Sun Tzu. The king's General shows that discipline has to be inculcated by being tough. He also makes the king understand that once he is empowered as General, he should not be questioned. It is my favourite because it echoes my strong belief that one should be uncompromising in work ethic and reminds me that a great leader is one who empowers his top management.

What do you tell yourself when you face insurmountable challenges? Typically, things where you need to make tough decisions?

It is funny, but I tell myself, 'All Izz Well,' as shown in '3 Idiots.' My approach is simple. If I can solve the problem, I won't worry about it. If I can't solve it, there is no point in worrying about it. I have also been lucky to always have wise counsel to tackle the tough problems, so it has been less challenging to that extent.

Do you feel stressed and overwhelmed? What do you do to cope with stress?

Yes, there are stressful times. I prefer to sleep well when I am stressed. I wake up with a fresh perspective after a good night's sleep. I have the gift of being able to switch on and off with sleep.

What is the single piece of advice you would like to give your peers?

Determine what your standards are and what your reference frame is. Then within that, live and let live. Strike a balance between minimalism and greed. Find your centre and stay there.

Have you thought about how you'd spend your time after retirement?

I have just started thinking about retirement and succession planning. Since I recently learnt how to play golf, I think I may like to do that if I find the right company. Perhaps, I need to develop some new hobbies now.

How do you measure yourself? Do you have quantitative or qualitative goals that you track and measure yourself against?

The measures have changed during the course of my life. Qualitatively, I want recognition. As mentioned, my family has been known in our village and community for its contributions, and I have always wanted to continue that.

What are a couple of words your family would use to describe you?

Lazy and Lucky :)

What is the one piece of advice you'd give your children?

I would tell my children to not run after name, fame or success. Like they say in the *Bhagvad Gita*, I tell them to do what they feel is good and that the rest will fall in place.

How do you approach difficult conversations and conflicts? Could you share what has worked for you?

As per psychometric evaluations, I am a very collaborative person. I reflect upon the conflict and often seek counsel from two to three people to get perspectives. I usually take the majority view. This has worked well for me. I don't need yes-men, and I am able to accept contradictory views to my own. However, I do work hard to surround myself with talented people whose counsel I then seek.

What was the last vocational or professional course you took, and did it help you?

The last course I've done is 'Family Office-how to sustain a family business,' at INSEAD. I recently also spoke to kids at the Indian School of Business about a case study based on our company. Both of these have been helpful in their own ways.

Do you have a connection with your hometown/place of birth/community?

Yes, I do have a deep connection with my hometown and community. I belong to a place called Buchireddypalem near Nellore. For decades, our ancestors have been well known in the locality. My family and I visit the place annually. I think it is very anchoring and important to have that connection with my hometown, and I feel lucky to have it.

What is the best form of giving back to the society you have experienced and would advocate for others?

Education. My grandfather and his brother did their bit by contributing to school and college education in our community, and I also believe it is the best thing that can be done for people in villages. I intend to do more of it once I have more time.

What is the legacy you wish to leave behind?

I always wanted to leave my mark. While the family was in the construction business, I got into dairy farming and took it on a big scale. I am glad I did that, and I wish to leave behind a sustainable organisation.

How do you define happiness? How often do you find yourself in this state?

For me, happiness is sleeping for 10 hours a day! Again, I am blessed to have the ability to sleep for long hours. It is a discipline I have inculcated, and it helps me stay focused and productive.

Any lesser-known facts about you that surprise people?

Most people think I am indeed lazy and lucky. However, they do not know that I do a lot of reading and deep thinking. There is a lot of strategy and hard work behind the outcomes that seem to come so easily to me.

What does spirituality mean to you, and how does it influence your approach to life?

It plays a significant role. As mentioned, there are sections of the *Bhagvad Gita* that are very relevant. I believe that there is a flow of nature that cannot be changed. So you do your best, be disciplined and go with the flow.

What role has education played in preparing you for the role you are now performing?

Education has played a key role. I did my engineering, and while the technical aspects of engineering are not with me now, I feel I have learned a structured approach to problem-solving. I can put everything into flow charts and analyse it. The other aspect of engineering that helped is that it was my first time staying away from the protected environment of my home. So I learned about the diversity of people and cultures and the soft skills required in life. Finally, college groomed us holistically and nourished us–it was not focused on academics alone.

Do you believe in discipline and routines, or are you a spontaneous person?

I believe that discipline is key to life. Whether it is sleep, professionalism, the delegation of power, or getting deeper into business, everything is on the foundation of the discipline.

Hyderabad's dairy diaries

Fostering South India's white revolution

Introduction

Prior to the 1980s, commercial milk was the sole initiative of a few government-run Co-operatives that controlled the supply of processed milk and a few value-added products such as ghee. This changed significantly in the decades that followed.

In 1983, Mr C.Bhaskar Reddy and D.Chandrashekher Reddy were pursuing dairy technology at a college in Kamareddy. They had dreams of pursuing higher studies in the United States, just like all of their other classmates. As fate would have it, though they got admission into US colleges, their visas were rejected. By 1986, together with two other friends, they decided to start their own dairy business in Hyderabad. Thus was born Creamline Dairy, more popularly known by its brand name: Jersey. Creamline entered the dairy industry when there were no private dairy companies in Hyderabad and started with milk products since commercial milk production was the imperative of the state-owned Andhra Pradesh Dairy Development Cooperative Federation Ltd. Milk was a supply-driven market with limited availability and little choice to the customer.

Luck turned in their favour when private dairies were allowed to enter the commercial milk market in 1991. Creamline began by giving a paper advertisement asking customers to respond if they were interested in packaged milk delivered at the doorstep. The four founders sat down and personally attended to over 400 phone calls in two-three days, taking down details of customer requests. Initial days involved going on their two-wheelers and hiring a few boys to fulfil the order deliveries. This was a critical success factor, as they understood the customer needs from a grass root level. In many ways, they forefronted the fresh milk supply with a door delivery option, direct to the consumer. From 1,300 litres delivered on the first day, they grew to a size of 30-35k litres daily by 1993-94.

They faced their share of challenges, especially when one of their biggest suppliers stopped delivering milk to them with ten days' notice. They then spent a lot more money procuring milk from other places, leading to a drop in quality and poor feedback from customers. However, after surviving such initial challenges, Creamline toughened and earned its success through sheer hard work. From humble beginnings in the early 90s, within three decades, the Jersey brand, now a part of Godrej Agrovet, has grown, diversified its product offerings and reported revenues of more than INR 1,000 crore for the year 2019-20.

A brief legislative history

The Operation Flood, India's White Revolution to be self-sustainable in milk production, is a well-known story. Dr Varghese Kurien, the story of Anand, the establishment of the National Dairy Development Board and the brand AMUL are also part of India's iconic dairy stories.

Let us take a quick look at the legislative history that shaped and impacted the dairy sector in India:

To give impetus to milk production via Operation Flood starting in 1968-69, the Government had

- Channelled imports through the National Dairy Development Board (NDDB) and
- Held the dairy sector under a licensing system through the Industrial Act 1951.

Their primary goal at the time was to promote all milk production through national and state cooperatives.

In 1991, there were sweeping reforms with liberalisation, and the government exempted the dairy sector from the Industrial Act 1951.

There was a 'flood' of interest from the private companies in the dairy sector following this change. However, complaints poured in from co-operatives about poaching by private companies, and to curtail this and establish quality standards, the government promulgated the Milk and Milk Products Order in 1992, under the Essential Commodities Act. This needed private companies to once again seek a license and set up their own milk sheds and procurement zones. The legislation has since undergone further changes in 2001 and 2003, and some restrictions have been eased. This has positively impacted the private dairy space in India.

Early Stage evolution in Hyderabad

One of the earliest players, Creamline Dairy, started operations under the brand name 'Jersey' in Hyderabad in 1989 as a micro-unit with smaller dairy products. By 1991, after the opening up of the liquid milk market to private players, Creamline was supplying about 50,000 litres of milk every day. Due to its customer focus, good quality of milk and convenience of door delivery, it saw success in the private market. A few other private companies entered during the 90s, though some of them could not sustain themselves. Indiana Dairy and Ravi Leela Dairy entered with big supplies of milk but couldn't invest in milk powder conversion equipment and quickly bled out and left the market. Mother Dairy, backed by the NDDB, had bulk milk and was a strong player in the market for some time. Guntur-based Sangam Dairy was an autonomous co-operative and supplied milk to various Southern India private dairies during 1993-94. Dodla dairy started in the Chittoor district in 1995, and within a couple of years, its operations took off well. They moved to Hyderabad in 2006. Heritage Dairy entered the space during the latter half of the 90s, procuring milk from Bangalore and Chittoor. After three-four years of struggle, they started seeing success with diversified products apart from milk. Tirumala Dairy started in Narsaraopet, Guntur and became a successful dairy company by the mid-2000.

Rapid expansion and consolidation

The late 90s and early 2000 were a phase of immense growth for the dairy industry. With an explosion in income levels, double-income families and several new grocery retail companies saw an increased appetite for dairy products other than milk, such as buttermilk, paneer, ghee, curd etc. The co-operatives were not able to keep up with the increasing brand equity of private dairy companies, which innovated and responded to the needs and preferences of customers quickly. Due to immense competition with co-operatives and amongst themselves, private dairies saw an increased opportunity in the value-added dairy products space to innovate in products, product marketing, packaging and creating brand equity. Also, during this phase, hundreds of chilling centres and plants were established across the state, aiding this rapid expansion. While there was speculation of consolidation by big multinational dairy companies, that did not happen to the extent expected. However, smaller local consolidations happened. During 2014-15, two big acquisitions happened, with Lactalis acquiring Tirumala Dairy and Godrej Agrovet acquiring a major stake in Creamline Dairy. Multinational companies continue to show interest in acquiring successful private dairy companies in the Indian market even to this day.

Impact at the bottom of the pyramid

Dairy farmers greatly benefited from this dairy sector expansion, with strong forward linkages. Private dairies helped the farmers by providing them with timely assured payments to their bank accounts, a strong support system for cattle health, feed management, breeding and best practices for optimal milk yield. Farmers also gained from having an option of being with the co-operatives or private dairy, whichever they found more beneficial. Overall, the sector is a big boon to the city and the state, enriching the lives of stakeholders across the board -farmers, dairy companies and consumers.

Way forward

The value-added products continue to be strong on both the demand and supply sides. India is the largest producer of cow milk in the world. A2 milk, which is milk that contains only A2 beta-casein, is purported to be more easily digestible. Indian breeds of bovines mostly produce A2 milk. The demand for A2 milk is undoubtedly growing, with strong micro players in the fray. These micro players often consist of urban professionals starting small dairy farms and supplying fresh organic milk to their neighbourhoods. This trend of fresh farm milk delivered directly to the home is gaining popularity. A few value-added products such as curd, butter and ghee are also being delivered farm fresh. A few of these companies are Kiaro Foods, Sids Farm, Charaka and Klimom. Some of these dairy farms are with Holstein-Friesian cows, while others offer A2 milk from native cow and buffalo breeds.

All dairy players, from the micro to the multinational, are looking at a robust future with the ever-increasing demand for milk and value-added milk products in India.

The Poultry Industry

All eggs in Hyderabad's basket

Introduction

The poultry sector in India consists of about 70% organized players and 30% unorganized players (known as backyard farming). About 67% of the market size is contributed by Broiler and 33% by Layer. India is ranked third in egg production and fourth in chicken meat production in the world.

The story of egg production was, however, very different for India in the 1960s. Back then, we weren't ranked even 90th in the world rankings for the production of eggs. A climb from there to the number three position is an arduous task and commendable.

DID YOU KNOW?

The credit for India's poultry revolution goes mainly to the late Padmashri Dr B.V. Rao, the founder of Venkateshwara Hatcheries Group, known popularly as Venky's, in 1971. It has since diversified into a global conglomerate that includes eggs, chicken, broiler and layer breeding, genetic research and poultry diseases diagnostic, poultry vaccine and feed supplements, vaccine production, bio-security products, poultry feed and equipment, and many more, becoming the largest fully integrated poultry group in Asia.

This company and its founder have a strong link to Hyderabad.

The Poultry revolution-how it started

The Venkateshwara group, registered in Pune, started in Telangana. Dr B.V. Rao, the father of poultry farming, was born in Hyderabad in 1935. After working different jobs, he joined the (then) Acharya NG Ranga University and attended a dairy and poultry farming training program. In the mid-1960s, Dr B.V. Rao used to take care of a few cows and chickens at the Osmania University (OU) campus and supply eggs and milk to a few professors. It so happened that during this time, America had sent a Mr Moore to India to train Indians on poultry breeding, and he happened to be at the OU campus. Watching the young and enthusiastic Dr B.V. Rao with his few chickens, he was impressed and decided to train him. Dr B.V. Rao then got employed with the American company that had sent Mr Moore and was trying to establish poultry practices and egg production in India. Subsequently, Dr B.V.Rao started working with Arbo Acres, and his boss at the time, Mr William Todd, had very high regard for his work. When Mr Todd later joined Babcock, USA, he offered the Babcock grandparent franchisee for India to Dr B.V. Rao and Mr C.Jagapati Rao.

Cutting back to 1965, Mr Chitturi Jagapati Rao, belonging to a small village in the East Godavari district of Andhra Pradesh, started a layer farm in Hyderabad with 6,000 layer birds. The Master's graduate from Jadavpur university was thinking of starting a medical shop in Kakinada at the time. The genesis for the poultry business idea came from his relative, who, when visiting from the US, struggled to get a handful of eggs for consumption in India. The relative believed in the immense potential of poultry in India, watching its success in Ohio in the US. He suggested that Mr Jagapati Rao try his hand at setting up something in India. Enthused by the suggestion, Mr Jagapati Rao entered into the layer business and went on to set up Srinivasa Hatcheries in Hyderabad.

As fate would have it, the two men got acquainted at a conference at Pune, where Dr B.V. Rao was working and residing. During the late 1960s, Mr Jagapati Rao and Dr.B.V. Rao became very close, travelling and supporting each other in understanding and building

Mettle

the poultry business in India. Dr B.V. Rao would keep trying to sell egg-laying chicks to Mr Jagapati Rao. By 1968-69 Dr B.V. Rao quit his job and decided to start a farm. Mr Jagapati Rao encouraged him to breed instead, and with Hy-lines exited from India at that time, a vacuum was created, giving them the space to start breeding. So in 1971, when Babcock agreed to franchise in India, the two friends were very excited. It was decided that Dr B.V. Rao would establish operations at Pune and take care of operations across India, whereas Mr Jagapati Rao focused on Andhra Pradesh.

The duo is responsible for Andhra Pradesh being the top producer of eggs and high ranking in poultry meat production in the country. The success and close bonding of the two men saw several milestones and developments in poultry farming for the country, including the establishment of the National Egg Coordination Committee (NECC) in Hyderabad in 1982.

The NECC was formed with the objective of having fair egg prices and fair terms for farmers across the country, a sort of cooperative similar to AMUL and milk co-operatives in the dairy sector. Their famous slogan was 'My egg, my price, my life.' In May 1982, the NECC was formally registered as a society under the Societies Registration Act. NECC stood strong in the face of traders who tried to break the price established by it. Today, over 25,000 farmers are registered with the NECC, which runs on voluntary contributions.

The critical success factor of both Venkateshwara and Srinivasa Hatcheries is their focus and commitment to improving farmers' lives. Dr B V Rao and Mr Jagapati Rao built an entire system for helping farmers manage the business, so much so that land and capital were the only criteria the farmers needed to worry about to start a poultry farm. For the capital, even the project reports used to be written up by these firms, to an extent where banks would be ready to approve projects if the reports were drawn up by either of these firms.

Huge challenges such as initial struggles with the import of birds, cold storage, transportation facilities for birds and eggs, battling bird diseases, availability of vaccines, managing costs and pricing of eggs dot this massive growth phase. The contribution of these two men in tackling the challenges and coming up with solutions is immense. Looking back, the climate and environment in which top poultry producers came up were just not conducive to poultry, for example, coastal Andhra and Namakkal in Tamil Nadu. Clearly, the commitment, risk-taking ability and focus of the entrepreneurs of these regions are what led to success in a fledgling market like poultry.

Immense growth potential

With a focus on protein for wholesome nutrition and development, the importance of the humble egg has shot up since it is one of the cheapest high protein options available for consumption in the country. There are numerous international and national players in the poultry business in India, as well as several smaller backyard farmers. The IMARC group estimates a 15% CAGR growth in the poultry industry over 2021-2026.

The domestic poultry industry is the fastest growing segment with a compound growth rate of 18%. Poultry meat is the most popular meat in India and has been receiving a significant boost through investments. The latest techniques of breeding, hatching, rearing and processing have transformed the poultry sector tremendously. The popularisation of hybrid poultry breeds, thanks to efforts by both government and private sectors, has brought in more profits.

Hyderabad is home to the biggest expo in the country

Poultry India, an international exhibition for the poultry industry, has had its annual show conducted in Hyderabad for several years now. The exhibition features the most innovative and reputed companies from the poultry sector, showcasing their businesses and interacting with potential partners, clients and investors. This event provides valuable information about the poultry industry, poultry feeds, poultry equipment, technology, chicken breeders, egg farming, poultry nutrition, animal health and international poultry production. It also offers the latest advancements in poultry research, science and technology, such as cages and feed milling.

Gaining ground-inching up to optimal egg consumption

The National Institute of Nutrition, based in Hyderabad, recommends an annual per capita egg consumption of 181 eggs. Telangana is the only state to achieve this, followed by Tamil Nadu, at 140 eggs per capita. Compared to other countries like China, at 300 eggs per capita and Japan, at 340 eggs per capita, this represents a much larger opportunity for India. The egg consumption definitely went up post-COVID, when a lot of doctors recommended taking protein in the diet in the form of eggs during their recovery from COVID. In terms of production, however, the Telangana state saw a dip in production post-pandemic, from 3.7 crores a day to 3.2 crores. About 2 crores of these eggs are used for domestic consumption, while the rest were sent to other states such as West Bengal, Maharashtra, Uttar Pradesh and Bihar. There are currently about 3,000-3,500 layer-producing farms in Telangana. Apart from Srinivasa Hatcheries, Hyderabad is home to Sneha Farms, also an industry leader. Sneha Farms has a benchmark unit - a fully automated processing facility with a capacity of 12,000 birds/hour.

In terms of overall poultry population, Telangana ranks third among states (behind Tamil Nadu and Andhra Pradesh) with a population of around 80 million birds at any given time.

Additionally, each egg increase in per capita consumption creates 35,000 jobs. Currently, Telangana's share in the country's egg production is nearly 13%. Similarly, in terms of meat consumption, the national average is four kg per capita, whereas the recommended level is eleven kg per capita, the world average being eighteen kg per capita. Thus, there is a huge scope for the growth of meat production. Overall, the poultry industry is expected to grow three times in the next 10-12 years.

Up and coming trends

Modernization of the Indian poultry industry is also on the cards, and the shift is happening gradually in terms of the adoption of new technology and equipment. India still houses most birds in open sheds, which is not the norm in other countries. The shift from open to environmentally controlled poultry houses has been happening for the last few years and is expected to accelerate in the near future. New technologies in terms of disease diagnosis, prevention and control are on the cards and taking shape gradually.

One important thing to notice is the shift from wet markets to hygienically processed meat. This shift is happening quite rapidly, and the processed meat industry is growing at 25% per annum compared to the overall poultry industry, which is estimated to be growing at around 10% per annum. The emergence of COVID has also added a trigger for people to shift from wet markets to hygienically processed poultry meat. The advent of online retailers like Licious, Tender cuts, Fresh to Home etc., has added momentum to this shift.

Food and Agri-processing

Agri processing

While the agricultural crop yield and related research studies are addressed by ICRISAT and Professor Jayashankar Telangana State Agricultural University, the processing of agricultural produce falls under the nutrition and food processing category. The National Institute of Nutrition (NIN) was established in Coonoor, Tamil Nadu, in 1918 and shifted to Hyderabad in 1958. The objective of NIN is to achieve optimal nutrition for vulnerable segments of the population. The NIN falls under the Indian Council of Medical Research (ICMR) and is its oldest and largest research centre, with significant contributions to the amelioration of several nutritional disorders in our population. It has attained global recognition for pioneering work in nutrition research, especially with respect to Protein Energy Malnutrition (PEM).

A look at agri-biotech and ICRISAT

Hyderabad is the proud home of two large campuses dedicated to the cause of improving agriculture and, thereby, farmers' lives while also solving problems of food and water management.

The first is Professor Jayashankar Telangana State Agricultural University at Rajendranagar, formerly the Acharya N G Ranga Agricultural University. The university was started in 1965 and inaugurated by the then Prime Minister Shri Lal Bahadur Shastri. It aims to serve the agricultural sciences through cutting-edge technologies and innovation across the spectrum of education, research and outreach to farmers. After the bifurcation, this remains the only State-run agriculture-focused university. It is credited with recognitions such as outstanding contribution to rice and maize research; innovation and research in seed production, forage crops and utilization and weed management; and in aiding commercialization of technologies through MoUs with private seed enterprises. It also runs two accredited labs, one in quality testing and another in testing for pesticide residue.

The International Crops Research Institute for the Semi-Arid Tropics, or ICRISAT, is on a mission to reduce poverty, hunger, malnutrition and environmental degradation in the drylands of Asia and Africa. The India headquarters is located in the vast campus at Patancheru, on 1,390 hectares of land. The research station offers an insight into the integration of agricultural sciences and research-for-development activities across the whole value chain – high-end science using germplasm from the genebank, genomics laboratory, phenotyping and genetic engineering facilities agribusiness centre, watershed management and crop production field experiments.

The institute and its scientists have consistently won awards, rewards and recognition for their exemplary contribution in the field of genetics, crop science, water management and agriculture. Two of the major breakthrough researches they have done relate to pearl millet and pigeon pea. The institute is one of the few agri research institutes that adopted an open-access policy for its publications.

Food processing

India has one of the largest food processing sectors in the world, and its growth prospects are immense. From an employment, output, and CAGR perspective, it checks all the boxes of a big, booming segment for India. The government has further provided an impetus by setting up 18 mega food parks and 134 cold chain projects to accelerate the development of the food processing supply chain.

Hyderabad is home to some popular food brands such as Priya Pickles and Bambino Industries, with the latter being the leading producer of vermicelli in India. Major multinational companies that have a presence in the state's food processing sector include Coca-Cola, ITC Ltd, Hatsun Agro Products and Plant Lipids.

Mettle

DID YOU KNOW?

Hyderabad - the Biscuit Capital of India

An *'Asli'* Hyderabadi biscuit that shot to fame is the Osmania biscuit, baked on demand for the last Nizam of Hyderabad, Mir Osman Ali Khan, who wanted a snack that was a little sweet and salty. Local bakeries such as Subhan, Nimrah, Niloufer, Karachi and Bahar are famous for their Osmania biscuits.

Dipping a biscuit into the quintessential cup of Indian tea, replete with milk and sugar, is an experience unto itself. Perhaps barring the current generation Z, most earlier generations will understand why this holds special regard in so many hearts. Apart from the traditional biscuits that are a staple Indian accompaniment with the *chai,* the bakery segment in India has really taken off. India is the 3rd largest biscuit manufacturer in the world, after the USA and China.

Biscuit manufacturing is a part of the larger food processing sector. In the 1980s, a few entrepreneurs started manufacturing their own brands of biscuits in Hyderabad. Slowly, the geographical factors were found to be conducive, and multinational companies started setting up their base in Hyderabad. Dukes is a famous homegrown biscuit brand of Hyderabad, and the Ampro biscuits (of Bambino group) factory in Uppal was a popular landmark to those growing up in the city. A whiff of the sweet-smelling biscuit factory en route to major schools in the Uppal and Ramanthapur area is a distinct memory for the children who grew up here in the 1980s and 1990s.

Hyderabad is known as biscuit capital due to the numerous contract manufacturers that are present in Katedan, manufacturing biscuits for Indian companies such as Parle, as well as for exports.

Aside from the big-name manufacturing establishments of biscuits that cater to domestic and export markets, there are bakery chains like the famous local Karachi Bakery, thousands of mom-and-pop stores, food trucks, and home-based cookies and cake businesses flourishing in the city.

Meat processing

India produces about 68 lakh tonnes of meat utilising about 10 crore meat animals such as cattle, buffaloes, sheep, goats and pigs and about 21 crore poultry.

While Hyderabad is most famous for its biryani, there is a lot of meat production and processing that also takes place in the city. It has several players in the organized meat processing and poultry segment.

The Indian Council of Agricultural Research (ICAR) - National Research Centre on Meat (NCRM) is located at Boduppal, Hyderabad. The institute was established with an aim to utilize livestock resources to provide meat and by-products to the growing population. It helps solve problems in meat and allied sectors through research, technology, and training and by maintaining a national information repository on meat and allied sectors.

Telangana has also achieved the distinction of being first in sheep rearing in the country, with about 93,000 tonnes of meat produced annually. The state has introduced incentivized sheep rearing by providing sheep distribution, supply of feed, insurance for sheep and deworming activities to ensure holistic support and boost to the segment. The worth of lamb and meat produced, about 93,000 tonnes, from this initiative is about INR 7,800 crore.

PART - III

Infrastructure Construction and
Building Materials Industry

Editor's Note on Infrastructure Construction and Building Materials Industry

Road trips have become much more popular after the Covid pandemic. When we drive on a road, highway, underpass or flyover - we are usually bothered by two things: the quality of the road and the traffic on it. Smooth roads and low traffic is every citizen's dream, and more so, a right because we all pay taxes that go into the construction of public infrastructure.

Public infrastructure is a wide-ranging segment that includes roads, highways, public transport, parks, irrigation systems, pipelines, government and municipal buildings and so on. Add to it the private infrastructure of commercial and residential properties, and you have a 360-degree experience as a citizen.

Undoubtedly, the place you live in dictates how you feel about the state of infrastructure of the country. Cities such as Hyderabad are blessed with amazing infrastructure facilities - wide roads, flyovers, the Nehru outer ring road, public transport, green parks, state-of-the-art public and private buildings, shopping malls, and commercial and residential complexes.

The Telangana government is investing in infrastructure through the development of special industry parks and economic zones, just as the central government is investing by building smart cities and national highways. This forms the backdrop for the infrastructure and construction industry.

Delving into research around the construction industry, I realized that a lot depends on the contractors executing construction projects on behalf of the government. The quality of the project, timeliness of delivery and the price at which the contract is executed are

Mettle

key features that determine the overall merit of the project. The infrastructure industry is supported by several allied industries, including building materials such as cement, ceramics, steel bars, etc. Numerous manufacturers and traders make their livelihoods in this industry. The number of design and architectural firms has exploded as commercial and residential construction increased significantly in an ever-expanding city landscape.

Profiled in this section are three industry leaders from infrastructure construction, cement and building materials segments in Hyderabad. They are at the helm of affairs in a tough business - resilient, innovative and focused on delivering their best. It takes a lot to execute massive projects like the construction of roads, highways and irrigation projects and to manufacture building materials that serve the sector. The dialogues with these business leaders reinforced that tremendous discipline, drive and execution excellence are essential ingredients to succeed in this segment. The best stand out, making a name for themselves at a national level, as have these three companies and their leaders. I hope you find the interviews and insights in this section as interesting as I did.

AAV Ranga Raju

Managing Director
NCC Ltd.
https://ncclimited.com/

A. A.V. Ranga Raju is a second-generation entrepreneur who is immensely proud to run an organization founded by his father, Padmashri Dr A.V.S. Raju. Mr Ranga Raju steered the organization through challenging times faced by the infrastructure and construction industry. Today, NCC Ltd. is a leader in this space, a title it earned through its focus on quality, commitment and timely completion. "Never hesitate to go the extra mile" is the strategy employed by Mr Ranga Raju, who believes in keeping client-centricity and value creation for stakeholders as the top priorities of the organisation.

Established In	Revenue for FY 20-21	Number of employees
1990	Rs **7,371** crores	**4,881**

Expertise	Order book
Civil construction for building and housing, water & environment, roads, electrical, mining, irrigation, power, railways and metals	**37,911** crores

INTERVIEW

Due to strict constraints surrounding COVID-19, this interview was not conducted in person. With immense gratitude, I present the interview of the successful MD and CEO of the NCC Group, Mr A.A.V. Ranga Raju.

So what is it that makes you spring out of bed each morning?

It is nothing but a will to serve the company and take it to greater heights.

What do you believe is the purpose of your life, personally?

It is to make life meaningful by serving humanity in general and my company in particular through employment generation and wealth creation.

At what age do you think you identified this, and what were your motivating factors?

I entered the family business at the age of 18. My main motivating factor was the work discipline of my father, Padmashri Dr A.V.S. Raju Garu.

Who or what has been the greatest influence in your life? A person, a book, a saying or a transformational moment you'd like to describe?

It is without any doubt my father, Dr A.V.S. Raju Garu. I have learned everything about life and business from him. He established NCC Ltd., and under his visionary leadership, we have been able to grow from strength to strength. Even today, I have the good fortune of having his counsel on things that matter the most.

They say the morning habits set a person's day up for success and productivity. What's the morning routine like before you get to work?

My morning routine starts with yoga, followed by other exercises. The discipline of morning fitness keeps me energetic and focused throughout the day.

What was the last most interesting book you read and why? What is a book you think everyone must read and why?

I think the *Bhagvad Gita* should be read by everyone because it teaches you how to balance your life.

What hobbies do you pursue currently, and how often do you find time for them?

I enjoy spending time with family and friends and watching cricket matches on TV. While work keeps me quite busy, I do manage to find spare time for my hobbies during weekends and holidays.

What do you think is the biggest lesson you learnt in 2020, the year of COVID?

It is equality. The situation has shown that we are all the same regardless of our religion, culture, customs and whether we are rich or poor. It has put nations across the world in crisis and taught us, as humanity, to come together to solve a problem of gigantic proportions.

What's your favourite quote of all time?

My favourite quote is "*Arise, awake, and do not stop until the goal is reached*" by Swami Vivekananda.

What do you tell yourself when you face insurmountable challenges? Typically, things where you need to make tough decisions?

I tell myself, "This too shall pass", and act with renewed vigour.

Do you feel stressed and overwhelmed? What do you do to cope with stress?

Yes, of course, stress is a part of one's life. To cope with stress, I divert my attention to other activities. I step back and away from the problem and come back once I am re-energized.

What is the single piece of advice you would like to give your peers?

Be patient and persistent.

Have you thought about how you'd spend your time after retirement?

I have not yet thought of retirement. Perhaps, when one enjoys what one is doing, retirement is not really on the mind.

How do you measure yourself? Do you have quantitative or qualitative goals that you track and measure yourself against?

I measure myself by looking at three factors: Energy, Work, Relationships

I have an inbuilt mechanism which tells me if I am going right on the above factors.

What are a couple of words your family would use to describe you?

Caring, loving and focused.

What is the one piece of advice you'd give your children?

Care for others, care for the elderly and be disciplined.

How do you approach difficult conversations and conflicts? Could you share what has worked for you?

I listen with a silent mind to the other point of view before making a decision. An open-minded, reflective approach has helped me overcome conflicts.

What was the last vocational or professional course you took, and did it help you?

I don't usually attend courses. My work is my greatest teacher.

Do you have a connection with your hometown/place of birth/community?

I belong to Antervedipalem, East Godavari district in Andhra Pradesh. I grew up there and had my education there. My visits to my native village strengthen the bond. I also take up some development activities in the area as part of CSR, and I am happy when I connect to my roots. The last time I visited my hometown was in 2020, and it made me realise the value of being connected to our roots.

What is the best form of giving back to the society you have experienced and would advocate for others?

I believe that charity begins at home. On a regular basis, I get involved in programs for uplifting the underprivileged. We have a trust named the Sirisha Trust. Through this, we provide shelter, food and education to orphans. Some of them have even joined NCC after their technical education. Yet another initiative is through the NCC Foundation, where philanthropic activities are undertaken.

What is the legacy you wish to leave behind?

The company I created, along with my father, i.e. NCC Ltd., is already a legend in the construction industry. I hope this legacy is carried forward by the next generation of leaders at NCC.

How do you define happiness? How often do you find yourself in this state?

It is a feeling of well-being, joy and knowing that you care for others.

Any lesser-known facts about you that surprise people?

That I am not well educated.

What does spirituality mean to you, and how does it influence your approach to life?

It means a search for meaning in life. It is an experience that touches me.

What role has education played in preparing you for the role you are now performing?

Education has played a limited role in preparing me for the role I am performing now. However, my work with peers and people down the level has made me who I am today.

Do you believe in discipline and routines, or are you a spontaneous person?

Discipline is my guiding force. However, certain decisions need to be made spontaneously based on intuition or insight. Thus, both are necessary and instrumental in getting things done.

K Ravi

Managing Director
NCL Industries Ltd.
https://nclind.com

K. Ravi is a second generation entreprenur, hailing from Polamaru, Bhimavaram. His father, K. Ramachandra Raju, tried a few entrepreneurial ventures before seeing success with Nagarjuna Cement. Ravi joined the business at a very young age after completing his Diploma in electrical engineering. He has since scaled NCL Industries to a diversified building materials company under his leadership, having fully taken over after his father retired. A workaholic to the core, he is extremely proud of the strong ties with all the promoter families, which have been maintained over the decades as NCL Industries grew.

Established In	Revenue for FY 20-21	Number of employees
1979	Rs **1,940** crores	**922**

Markets	Expertise	Cement Capacity (Tonnes)
Pan India	Cement, particle boards and doors	**2,700,000**

Cement dealers	Particle board dealers
2243	**350**

INTERVIEW

I walked in on a summery afternoon into the elegantly appointed offices of NCL Industries Ltd. Glass doors and wood-panelled interiors greeted me, and the overall feeling was classy corporate. I was told that many aspects of the interiors were personally looked into by Mr K. Ravi himself. I was shown into his office at the appointed time, and the conversation flowed over cups of coffee. Mr K. Ravi started his story by talking about his father's humble beginnings, who worked at a chemical factory in Srikakulam. He subsequently evolved into an entrepreneur in Hyderabad, moving from effluent treatments to cement to building materials. Mr Ravi spoke freely of how he learned so much from his father, even as they were in conflict over certain topics, and how he taps into his philosophy even today whenever he feels troubled. He spoke about how his company was bold in bringing innovative products through collaborations but how the market always took a long to respond to them. One thing he holds dear is that none of the promoter families has exited the company. Their ties have been strong through the decades, and several next-generation members have joined the business and are actively involved in it. He believes this is due to strong fundamental bonds that cannot be dictated to by investors or anyone else. Candid, open and simple to the core, Mr Ravi is a visionary with a passion for the company's legacy. Read on to learn more about him.

So what is it that makes you spring out of bed each morning?

The livelihood of some 3,000 families depends on my company. The pandemic certainly had me worried. After 40 years of struggle, I wanted to ensure we did our best to survive the pandemic. Keeping the company going and growing is what makes me spring out of bed each day.

What do you believe is the purpose of your life, personally?

I believe that doing nothing is a burden to society, and as long as one is capable, one must do something for society. The business generates money, taxes for the government, employment for people, and service to society. I believe my purpose is to keep doing what I can.

At what age do you think you identified this, and what were your motivating factors?

After I finished my studies, my father wanted me to join the business. I just managed to complete my education, and I soon accompanied him. Ever since I have taken the business as my purpose.

Who or what has been the greatest influence in your life? A person, a book, a saying or a transformational moment you'd like to describe?

Undoubtedly, it is my father. Even today, when I run into problems with the business, I think about how he would have approached it, and that helps me in finding answers. My father had very humble beginnings, and after failing at a few ventures initially, he found success with the effluent treatment plants, which we still operate as part of our company. My father always used to say that we came with nothing, so we have nothing to lose. That helps me put things in perspective at all times.

They say the morning habits set a person's day up for success and productivity. What's the morning routine like before you get to work?

If I don't have a lot to do in the morning, I like to go golfing. If I am up late into the night or have early commitments at work, I skip golf and come early to the office.

What was the last most interesting book you read and why?

I stopped reading books long back. Once in a while, I manage to read a few, and these are more real-life stories. I can recall Lee Iacocca's autobiography and Sudha Murthy's compilation of real-life incidents.

Which book do you think everyone must read and why?

I don't have any such recommendations.

What hobbies do you pursue currently, and how often do you find time for them?

I love golfing and playing with my dogs. I play with my dogs every day, and for golfing, pre-COVID, I used to go about three times a week.

What do you think is the biggest lesson you learnt in 2020, the year of COVID?

That survival drives you to work very hard. I did not take any break from work. I put my health at risk and travelled everywhere.

What's your favourite quote of all time?

Keep Growing

What do you tell yourself when you face insurmountable challenges? Typically, things where you need to make tough decisions?

I tell myself to face the situation head-on and not run away. Business is full of commitments, and I think one needs to always provide answers. Even during our most challenging times, I always gave answers. I think decisions must be taken even if they are tough. Postponing taking of decision is similar to indecision, and it is bad. So, to sum it up, I just take the challenge head-on and take a decision.

Do you feel stressed and overwhelmed? What do you do to cope with stress?

I spend time with my grandchildren or play with my dogs.

What is the single piece of advice you would like to give your peers?

Take business as serious business and be focused!

Have you thought about how you'd spend your time after retirement?

I'd like to continue golfing and, of course, playing with my dogs

How do you measure yourself? Do you have quantitative or qualitative goals that you track and measure yourself against?

We grew from less than INR 100 crores in revenue to about INR 1,500 crore in revenue over the decades. I never had any strict measures but believed in always growing. I believe in seizing opportunities whenever they arise.

What are a couple of words your family would use to describe you?

Short tempered, bossy and demanding :)

What is the one piece of advice you'd give your children?

My children are grown up, are educated and have seen the world. I now take advice from them rather than give them advice.

How do you approach difficult conversations and conflicts? Could you share what has worked for you?

When there are conflicts, I generally take my time. In case the conflict is aggravating, I take even more time. I try not to be aggressive or criticise. I don't react or respond to things that don't need attention.

What was the last vocational or professional course you took, and did it help you?

The last course I took, so to speak, was going to a Buddhist Dharmashala for meditation. I, however, did not enjoy it.

Do you have a connection with your hometown/place of birth/community?

I belong to a place called Polamuru near Bhimavaram. Most of the families there are involved in agriculture. Due to land reforms, many families lost their lands. Slowly, many of these people migrated to Hyderabad. Since my father also left his hometown early in life, we don't have a deep connection with the place as such. However, we are closely connected with the community of people who migrated to Hyderabad.

What is the best form of giving back to the society you have experienced and would advocate for others?

I think running a business is the best form of giving back to society. Business and industry form the backbone of the country. They generate employment and taxes. There isn't a better way in which one can build the country.

What is the legacy you wish to leave behind?

Legacy is the business which we have promoted. Promoters should not be focused on making money for themselves. They should not be afraid of failures and must make bold investments. They should think of doing things to help others. That is a true legacy.

How do you define happiness? How often do you find yourself in this state?

My family being able to eat on time and live comfortably is happiness for me. Not having to beg in life is happiness. Happiness comes from having all the bare essentials met.

Any lesser-known facts about you that surprise people?

I am not as serious as people think I am. I always communicate with a sense of humour.

What does spirituality mean to you, and how does it influence your approach to life?

Spirituality is very simple for me, really. It means being a good human being and not cheating anyone. My father used to say that God was created by human beings to keep society in order. Hence, I do not believe in God.

What role has education played in preparing you for the role you are now performing?

Education has played only a small role. Almost everything I learned in business was through my father, and that is what has helped me a lot.

Mettle

Do you believe in discipline and routines, or are you a spontaneous person?

Discipline and routines are very important. Hard work is very important to me. It is not possible to achieve success without discipline.

Jalandhar Reddy

Executive Director
KNR Constructions Ltd.
http://www.knrcl.com/

K. Jalandhar Reddy is a second-generation entrepreneur from Dammannapeta village in the Warangal district. KNR Constructions was started by his father, K. Narasimha Reddy, in 1995. After completing their Bachelor's in computer engineering in Bangalore, he gave up an opportunity to study for his Masters's degree overseas. Instead, Jalandhar joined his father's business and learnt the business from the basics. He slowly worked his way up the organization. Today, he manages and executes massive projects with excellence and runs the business with utmost passion. Constructing quality roads, highways, and building irrigation projects and other infrastructure is his way of contributing to the nation.

Established In
1995

Revenue for FY 20-21
Rs **2,702** crores

Number of employees
2,162

Markets present
11 States

Expertise
Construction of roads, highways, bridges and flyovers.
Irrigation projects and urban water infrastructure management, and agriculture

Road projects (km)
7500

Order book
7118 crore

INTERVIEW

It was a rainy afternoon when I parked my car at the headquarters of KNR Constructions Ltd. Right from the entrance to the elevators, I could sense the COVID-19 safety precautions being taken. Soon after the guard checked the temperature, I noticed toothpicks inserted on a piece of thermocol outside the elevators to be used to press the buttons. Inside the elevator was a simple instruction on how to dispose of used toothpicks. It went to show how one can be simple and thorough in creating effective processes.

Mr Jalandhar Reddy's large office room had a big screen CCTV showing the employee floors in front of his eyes, and behind him were his favourite quote and a few simple knick-knacks.

Mr Jalandhar comes across as a simple and focused man who takes his work's utility very seriously. Having had an opportunity to pursue further education in the US, he gave it up to join his father's business, upon his mother's guidance. And he largely credits both his parents for his successfully scaled-up business.

During one of the questions, he demonstrated how he can easily divert himself during stressful times by looking through the window of his office from where he sees the sky, the metro rail, and the buzzing city life. We wrapped up the interview in close to two hours, consciously coming back to the questions asked and refocusing on the interview to achieve our goal. I hope reading it is as enjoyable as taking the interview was.

So what is it that makes you spring out of bed each morning?

I love my work, the impact it makes on the places where we build and construct, and the contribution we make to the country. I believe in doing a job not just well but with passion. I take quality in my work very seriously, and I am proud of everything we do. I thus look forward to fulfilling my responsibilities each day.

What do you believe is the purpose of your life, personally?

To do my best for the company. To raise my children in a good environment and make them useful to the country. To continue to serve my country as I do now by building roads and irrigation projects. To excel each day and do better than the previous day. This is my purpose.

At what age do you think you identified this, and what were the motivating factors?

I think I identified this about two years after joining the company.

Who or what has been the greatest influence in your life? A person, a book, a saying or a transformational moment you'd like to describe?

My father is my guru and my everything. He made me an engineer and an entrepreneur. The best part was that he did it without forcing me. He ensured I got trained in every aspect of the business. Even though he could see that I was keen on pursuing something else, such as going to the US for higher education, he did not forbid me from it. My mother is the one who advised me to join the business and help him. And I am so glad I did. I learned so much from him, and I owe my entire success to my father.

They say the morning habits set a person's day up for success and productivity. What's the morning routine like before you get to work?

There is a lot to do in a day, and I believe in "Early to bed, Early to rise." I wake up at 05:00 am and start my exercise routine at 05:30 am. While working out at the gym, I speak to all my managers at various sites and get a status update. This is how my days typically start.

What was the last most interesting book you read and why?

I don't read a lot of books, to be honest.

Which book do you think everyone must read and why?

The *Bhagvad Gita*. More than reading, I think implementing small aspects of it is important. For example, I was a bit sceptical about expanding my operations in North India. But after reading some relevant portions of the Gita, I got the message of being brave and removing fears. So I did that. I applied for tenders in the North, and now I am proud to say we have pan-India operations.

What hobbies do you pursue currently, and how often do you find time for them?

I like swimming and spending time with my kids. Earlier I used to play badminton but cannot find time for it these days.

What do you think is the biggest lesson you learnt in 2020, the year of COVID?

We are learning to live in tough times and do our best in testing times. We are in situations where things can change rapidly, and we must manage risks all the time. With time-bound commitments, I stay solution-oriented rather than problem-oriented.

I think one must always keep themselves updated and prepared. One must take precautions but move on and not stop. I did not stop working during COVID-19. I took the necessary precautions and got the necessary permissions, but the work did not stop.

What's your favourite quote of all time?

(Shows it from right behind his chair)

Have Faith. God never shuts one door without opening another.

What do you tell yourself when you face insurmountable challenges? Typically, things where you need to make tough decisions?

To be brave, focused and updated. To always have the P&L margin focus and manage costs efficiently. I am also open to listening to new ideas from my teams and even external service providers. The focus has to be on solutions to the challenges and not the challenges themselves.

Do you feel stressed and overwhelmed? What do you do to cope with stress?

Yes, for sure. There is stress in running a business enterprise. There are two causes of stress, the first is an overload of work, and the second is the inability to address problems. One must be brave and solve problems one by one. Thinking about solutions is a good way to reduce stress. At times, I look outside my window from my cabin. Looking at the expansiveness of the sky and the roads outside relieves me of stress. Sometimes I spend time with my parents or kids. Once my mind is calm again, I focus on problem-solving.

What is the single piece of advice you would like to give your peers?

I don't really have the advice to give to my peers. However, I do believe that we are all doing something for the public. This is our prime duty. We must build good and safe roads and maintain them properly. It is a public service and should be taken seriously.

Have you thought about how you'd spend your time after retirement?

After retirement, I would like to spend more time doing charitable services. I mean actual physical work that is charitable. I would also like to do more devotional work. Once I am free from business, I will have time to focus on these.

How do you measure yourself? Do you have quantitative or qualitative goals that you track and measure yourself against?

I don't measure myself. I am confident in what I do. If I take wrong decisions, whenever possible, I reverse them. By God's grace, I have not taken decisions that have negatively impacted the company. I never had specific goals for myself. I just wanted to do the best for the company.

What are a couple of words your family would use to describe you?

Hard worker.

What is the one piece of advice you'd give your children?

I tell them to be focused and efficient in whatever they do. Depth of knowledge is very important. I want them both to grow and be their own person. They are young, and I want them to be physically active and focus on their studies. If they read something, I want them to know it entirely and deeply.

How do you approach difficult conversations and conflicts? Could you share what has worked for you?

In my case, the difficult conversations are when I run behind schedules I have committed to the government. I am usually calm and talk to them about it. In case we cannot resolve the conflict, we can go to arbitration.

Internally there are no conflicts in the organisation. I take people's input, but I take final decisions. As a listed company, we must ensure that we do our best for our shareholders and investors.

What was the last vocational or professional course you took, and did it help you?

I have not taken any course as such. In most situations, taking advice from my mother or father has helped me.

Do you have a connection with your hometown/place of birth/community?

Yes, I do. I belong to Dammannapeta, near Wardhannapet taluka headquarters, close to Warangal. We have renovated my grandparents' home and performed CSR activities for my father's village. We go and live at our grandparents' home whenever we can.

What is the best form of giving back to the society you have experienced and would advocate for others?

My father hails from a village where facilities are poor. So, we adopted the village and have improved it in terms of public health, schooling, etc. I think education is the way forward, and therefore, we try and do as much as we can for schools. I strongly believe that the country should have a lot more literates. We are also looking to create water facilities for farmers in and around our village.

What is the legacy you wish to leave behind?

Our company has been running for 45 years, and I want it to sustain itself. My father gave it to me, and I started my way at the bottom before being at the helm. The vision is to keep it running for at least 100 years. It is easy to quit this business. But staying in it, building quality roads is a good service to the public. So, I take my job very seriously. I pay attention to every minute detail. This is the legacy I wish to leave for my company.

How do you define happiness? How often do you find yourself in this state?

I love my job, and I am happy most of the time. As long as things go well, I do not want to divert myself. I set my targets for the company happily and then go about achieving them. I have a deep conviction in what I do. Completing each project to the best ability and quality, having my own barometer to measure myself is very important. In all of these, I find my happiness.

Any lesser-known facts about you that surprise people?

I am very updated in my field. I have my own ideas, and in most meetings, people are surprised by how much I am updated and can contribute in terms of thoughts and ideas.

What does spirituality mean to you, and how does it influence your approach to life?

Spirituality is everything! Belief must always be complete and full. I believe that God exists. My spirituality gives me peace of mind.

What role has education played in preparing you for the role you are now performing?

Education is fundamental, and we need the experience to teach us beyond the basics. Learning is an ocean, and I always strive to keep myself updated in my field.

Do you believe in discipline and routines, or are you a spontaneous person?

Discipline is everything, and I fully believe in it.

Infrastructure Construction and Building materials

Fundamentally strong

Brief History

The construction of the Nagarjunasagar dam across River Krishna in Nalgonda district in 1955 is the first historical milestone of infrastructure construction in the state combined with Andhra Pradesh then. Inaugurated by the then Prime Minister Jawahar Lal Nehru, the 124-mt tall and 1.6-km long dam is also the second largest reservoir in India. The construction took more than a decade, and the dam was inaugurated in 1967, following which a hydel power plant was built and commissioned in 1978.

Everyone who came to the area to participate in the construction project started looking for jobs after the completion of the project. This, combined with a growing interest by entrepreneurs in the infrastructure construction industry, led to the boom in the region.

National scenario

The next big growth phase witnessed across the country was due to the National Highway Development Project (NHDP), which was started in 1998 by then Prime Minister Atal Bihari Vajpayee. The southern region played a key role in the project. Phase I of the NHDP, known as the Golden Quadrilateral project, was started with the aim of connecting the four metropolitan cities - Delhi, Kolkata, Mumbai and Chennai. This massive Phase I of the project concluded in 2012. In the meantime, several other phases have been underway, such as the construction of expressways, mass rapid transit systems, connectivity of state capitals, and improving city networks to ease traffic congestion, irrigation projects, and many more.

Large construction companies such as L&T grew bigger, and smaller companies started growing and getting listed. At times, the listed companies got more focused on getting order books fulfilled to appease market analysts and investors and waged aggressive bidding wars. During the rule of the UPA government, the industry, while it grew, also faced challenges such as policy paralysis. The government opened up the Build-Operate-Transfer (BOT) model for major infrastructure projects, via which private entities finance, build and operate the projects for 20-30 years, after which the project is handed back to the government. There was a lot of politics within this space. Growth in private space was oriented towards profitable ventures such as highways, ports, airports, power plants etc. and not in basic infrastructures such as elementary schools, toilets, water supply and drainage systems. This was the backdrop of the industry through the late 90s and early 2000s.

Hyderabad witnesses substantial growth

With BOT projects and industrial parks, highways, airports and other government-sponsored infrastructure projects, the growth of the sector took off in Hyderabad. The next wave in construction got fuelled by the arrival of several multinational companies and the creation of special economic zones in Hyderabad, taking up massive spaces in commercial real estate around the city. With these companies employing several thousands of people, the demand for residential housing also went up considerably. Allied sectors of building materials such as cement, ceramic tiles and sanitary ware mushroomed, and several smaller companies established themselves or expanded into this region. The early 2000s saw the expansion of the Hi-Tech City and Gachibowli area, with several multinational companies and residential complexes, the ISB, and several private schools coming up. The residential and commercial market kept growing near this belt and has expanded and exploded to areas adjacent to and connected by the Jawahar Lal Nehru Outer Ring Road.

Back during the period 2006-2010, it could be said that Hyderabad was the infrastructure capital of India. The barriers to entry were few.

Profit margins were well protected, as most companies received a 10% advance before commencement of work.

Local companies such as SEW Infrastructure, Megha Engineering and the Nava Yuga group bagged contracts for the Kaleshwaram Lift Irrigation Project. Construction equipment manufacturers such as Kobelco and Atlas Copco invested more in the Hyderabad region, and this sub-segment saw a lot of other national and multinational players such as L&T, Volvo, ACE, and Universal, JCB, Doosan, Caterpillar, Mahindra and Sandvik. The GMR group constructed Hyderabad's international airport, which was inaugurated in 2008. Commercial and residential real estate saw a flood of developers such as IVRCL, Madhucon Granites Ltd., Gayatri Projects Ltd., My Home Group, Nava Bharat Ventures Ltd., PVR Developers, Lanco Group, Raheja Group, L& T, Ramky Group and Aparna Constructions.

Telangana is ranked tenth in the Logistics Ease Index, with a scope to improve its rail and terminal infrastructure facilities. Limited availability of warehouses and lack of sufficient rail and air freight facilities make the industries here depend on other states and ports for some of their export activities. The state has, however, done well in the safety and security of cargo during transportation and at its terminals. With the right public-private partnership model to create more aggregation and disaggregation points for cargo movement and skill development for this sector, significant improvements are possible.

A favourable ecosystem

The ecosystem for building, construction and infrastructure is very robust in the state. With a CAGR of 10-12% estimated during FY 2017-18 and a flurry of infra projects, the sector has a strong presence and is continuing to grow.

There are several advantages and favourable factors for Telangana and Andhra Pradesh that are conducive to the infrastructure and building materials industry. There are more than 50 small and large infrastructure companies, 400 civil contractors, 1,000 builders and

50 cement plants. Institutions such as National Cement, Construction and Building Material (NCCBM) and the National Academy of Construction are based out of Hyderabad and play a key role in nurturing the growth of the industry in the city.

Challenges and closures

While there was enormous growth, on the one hand, the industry faced several challenges. Some of the key problems that plagued this industry were high-interest rates, high inflation, payment cycle deterioration, and liquidity crunch, leading to corporate debt restructuring. Some companies exchanged debt for equity, with lenders becoming owners. The dilution of the promoter's stake did not augur well with clients. At times, the clients got jittery, performance guarantees got invoked, and generally, things got worse. These reasons led to the closure, liquidation or insolvency of several companies.

In 2016, IVRCL became insolvent and was acquired by Gabs Megacorp in 2019. The GVK Constructions group was mired in controversy over the money laundering case related to its airport management vertical, which is still to be resolved at this point in time. In 2018, Lanco Infratech, headquartered in Gurgaon, was declared bankrupt. Kolkata-based Simplex Infrastructures Ltd. has been declared an NPA by a consortium of banks. However, a few top companies such as NCC Ltd., KNR Constructions Ltd., Gayatri Projects Ltd. and Megha Engineering from Hyderabad have survived the tough times.

The road ahead

After the first wave of COVID-19 slowed by the start of 2021, things started improving for the industry. Low-interest rates and improved payment cycles indicate that things are improving. COVID loans were given to infrastructure companies. Commercial real estate picked up, and gated communities in the residential market are doing well.

In March 2020, the National Highway Authorities of India disbursed about INR 10,000 crore through online payments to ensure it has no pending dues. New measures mandate that if a contractor has done work and is certified, then payment shouldn't be withheld. The NHAI has also awarded 1,330-km length projects worth INR 47,289 crore during Apr-Sep 2020.

All of these measures, along with a committed spend of INR 1.18 lakh crore as per the Union Budget of 2021-22 on road transport and highway infrastructure, further indicate immense growth potential for this industry.

Cement and Building materials–Robust, Strong and Forging ahead

Building materials such as cement, ceramic and steel are in abundant supply in the state. There are a number of established players in the segment, and the state government has implemented several measures to attract more investments, both domestic and international, to Hyderabad. The Metro, MMTS, SRDP and other infrastructure projects in the city are a big boost to the sector. Further, several SEZs, bio parks, technology parks, financial districts, pharma city, IT hubs and startup incubators planned in the city are growth drivers. Additionally, the presence of several big multinational companies as employers and their employees as residential customers has added to the growth of the segment.

Companies such as Hyderabad Industries Limited (now part of the CK Birla group), Visaka Industries, NCL Industries and Kirby Building Systems are prominent players in the building materials segment.

India is the second largest producer of cement in the world after China, with an installed cement capacity of approximately 545 million tonnes. India's cement plants are some of the greenest in the world, at par with Japan in energy consumption and adoption of green practices.

30% of India's limestone reserves are situated in Andhra Pradesh, Karnataka and Telangana alone, and thus South India has the potential to become a cement hub for both the domestic and export markets.

Of the 150 MT cement market in South India, about 50% of the capacity is in Andhra Pradesh and Telangana alone, with 50-60 key players established in these two states. Some prominent ones are Sagar Cements, Penna Cements, Nagarjuna Cements, Priya Cements, Bharati Cements (flagship brand of French group Vicat), Orient Cements, etc.

Cement production is boosted by the significant infrastructure spending committed to by the Government of India. Metro rail projects and expressways, smart city projects, highways etc., have driven the demand for high-quality and quantity of cement. State investments such as skyways, flyovers, parks, avenue plantations, etc., also drive up consumption. The city has also witnessed a big boom in commercial property development by big players such as RMZ, Embassy Group, CBRE and others, as well as in residential property by players such as Ramky Infrastructure, Aparna Constructions, Prestige, Jayabheri group, etc.

PART - IV

Aerospace and Defence Industry

Editor's Note on Aerospace and Defence Industry

Nine out of ten children, when asked what they want to be when they grow up, will probably say 'pilot'. Flying aircraft in the blue skies is a fascinating dream for young minds. In fact, Generation Z and beyond might want to fly rockets into space since they are exposed to broader horizons. However, only after growing up does one realize that there is so much depth and vastness to making aircraft, building warships and missiles. I was captivated by the facts and stories I discovered upon researching the aerospace and defence industry in Hyderabad. The magnitude and breadth of its presence, and the recent developments that attracted many entrepreneurs and multinationals alike, are a boon for the city.

The industry originated with the establishment of a few laboratories of the DRDO (Defence Research & Development Organisation), an agency of the Ministry of Defence in Hyderabad. The city was viewed as strategic, located centrally in the southern part of India, away from the borders of the country. The pioneering work of the esteemed DRDO labs paved the way for precision engineering and component manufacturing in Hyderabad. It is a matter of pride that former President of India, Dr A.P.J. Abdul Kalam spent a lot of time in Hyderabad and established the Missile laboratories DRDL and RCI here.

Most of the fuel for the defence industry's expansion came from government initiatives in the 1960s, 70s and 80s. Bharat Dynamics Ltd, Hindustan Aeronautics Ltd, Ordnance Factory, Mishra Dhatu Nigam Ltd. etc., were the PSUs established in Hyderabad, leading to the development of ancillary industries. Precision engineering, batteries, devices and components for use in defence and aerospace are examples of a few such ancillary industry segments.

Mettle

The city's previous airport at Begumpet was an ordinary terminal. International flights were few and far in Hyderabad. In fact, the runway was specially extended to accommodate Air Force One when President Bill Clinton landed in the city in 2000. Less than a decade later, in 2008, the magnificent and world-class Rajiv Gandhi International airport was inaugurated at Shamshabad. The GMR group built this airport and made it India's first integrated cargo terminal with international, domestic and pharma zone cargo management capabilities. Several global equipment manufacturers in the aviation industry have since established operations in Hyderabad, and the Telangana government is further incentivising foreign and domestic investments.

This section profiles an entrepreneur of one of Hyderabad's pioneering defence and aerospace companies. He is an ambitious business leader who still works every day, even in his seventies. Spirituality and meditation have taken priority at this stage in life, but he finds a great amount of zeal in looking after the day-to-day operations of his expanding business. The aerospace and defence industry needs dedication, discipline and specialized knowledge to succeed. I hope you enjoy the interview and the industry insights that follow.

Aerospace Production

Dr Amar Nath Gupta

Chairman & Managing Director
Premier Explosives Ltd.
www.pelgel.com

Dr Amar Nath Gupta is a first-generation entrepreneur hailing from Jammu. A student of the Indian School of Mines, Dr Amarnath was content as an employee with Singareni Collieries. A chance conversation and a decision to take a leap of faith turned him into an entrepreneur, and he founded Premier Explosives in 1980. The company is one of the pioneering and leading ones in Hyderabad's growing aerospace and defence industry. Starting off as a small-scale enterprise that manufactured commercial explosives, Premier has since evolved, expanded and specialised in critical areas such as propellant manufacturing for missiles and high-energy materials for the defence and aerospace industry.

Established In
1980

Revenue for FY 20-21
152 crores

Number of employees
975

Order book
464 crores

Expertise
High energy materials for defence, space, mining and infrastructure industries. Solid propellants and various other products for use in rockets, missiles and satellites

INTERVIEW

On the noon of a Saturday, I walked into the office of Premier Explosives Ltd., located in a small lane in a predominantly residential locality. Due to COVID, it was rather quiet and desolate. After a half-hour wait, I entered the cabin of Dr Amar Nath Gupta, which was well-lit and spacious. He was in conversation with some of his staff, still so deeply involved in the details of the company's day-to-day operations. Professionally, business continues to be his priority, while personally, his deeper interests are in meditation, prayer, and spirituality.

So what is it that makes you spring out of bed each morning?

Every day is an opportunity as you can't be sure to wake up again the next day. Therefore, all I want when I wake up is to have a successful day.

What do you believe is the purpose of your life, personally?

The purpose of my life is to stop rebirths and attain 'moksha'.

At what age do you think you identified this, and what were the motivating factors?

I think when I was younger, my purpose was to be a successful entrepreneur. Now at this age, I have reset my goals.

Who or what has been the greatest influence in your life? A person, a book, a saying or a transformational moment you'd like to describe?

My work with Premier Explosives and spiritually, the **Bhagvad Gita** are the biggest influences in my life.

However, I must share the story of how I started Premier Explosives. Life changed for me with an interview at midnight with Mr C.N. Sastri, Chairman of Singareni Collieries. Singareni had a shortage of explosives, and Mr Sastri asked me if I could make the explosives. He gave me a chance to transform myself from an employee to an entrepreneur. I was employed at Indian Explosives Ltd. in Calcutta at that time. I immediately agreed and sent my resignation letter by fax. Mr Sastri asked me how much land I needed and helped me secure 700 acres. Regarding the name - I saw a calendar or something and just decided to name the company 'Premier Explosives.' The company had meagre beginnings, and I am proud of what we have now accomplished.

They say the morning habits set a person's day up for success and productivity. What's the morning routine like before you get to work?

I wake up around 03:30, or 04:00 am and spend an hour doing *'dhyaan'*, thinking of God consciously. I am trying to work my way up there. Sometimes I go back to sleep and wake up around 06:30 am. I then think about problem-solving, check my emails, have my tea and get to the office by 09:00 am. I use the morning to plan my daily appointments and meetings. It makes for productive days at work.

What was the last most interesting book you read and why?

The Bhagvad Gita. In general, I read a lot. During every travel, I used to buy books and finish them en route itself. Most authors I read, I would have read their entire collection.

Which book do you think everyone must read and why?

I think everyone should read the Gita. It gives a lot of wisdom. It is also the most misquoted and misinterpreted book. Of all the interpretations, the most interesting one is by Adgadanand JI Maharaj.

What hobbies do you pursue currently, and how often do you find time for them?

My hobbies are photography, writing poetry and listening to music. These days, I do *'dhyaan'* every day and enjoy doing it in my spare time.

What do you think is the biggest lesson you learnt in 2020, the year of COVID?

I think the biggest lesson was survival. We all learned how to survive a bad year. For Hyderabad, delayed and extended monsoons also took the city under water. But, we all learned to be resilient in that year.

What's your favourite quote of all time?

My favourite quote is "burn your boats." If you want to achieve something, all your exits must be closed. Then you can focus on your goal. Don't look for shortcuts. In negotiations, though, it is the opposite. Don't close all the doors when you are negotiating, so you can always go back if needed.

What do you tell yourself when you face insurmountable challenges? Typically things where you need to make tough decisions.

Life itself is challenging. Whatever obstacles come in life, you need to overcome them one by one. If you think of them as tasks, you just need to take action and tackle them one by one. If you think of them as obstacles, they are bigger, and you need to think of how to overcome them.

Do you feel stressed and overwhelmed? What do you do to cope with stress?

If you take life in stride, then there is no stress. I get upset only when I cannot do anything. Stress becomes an obstacle, so it is best avoided.

What is the single piece of advice you would like to give your peers?

Believe in yourself. If you don't have faith, you will certainly fail.

Have you thought about how you'd spend your time after retirement?

Yes, I would like to read and complete all the things that I couldn't do. I would like to spend time reading and doing *dhyaan*.

How do you measure yourself? Do you have quantitative or qualitative goals that you track and measure yourself against?

You can only compete with yourself. If you are doing better than you were, then you are doing well. Looking at others does no good to anyone.

What are a couple of words your family would use to describe you?

Hard-working and works to perfection. Sincere and cares for humanity.

What is the one piece of advice you'd give your children?

Nothing is impossible if you have faith in yourself and plan for it dispassionately. You should do your SWOT analysis. If you plan, you can do many things. Often, not planning leads to failure.

How do you approach difficult conversations and conflicts? Could you share what has worked for you?

Ideally, conflicts should not arise. If you approach problems such that there is no conflict, then it is helpful. One can have internal conflicts, but not with others. When approaching these issues, it's best to be right, firm and straightforward. Never try and take advantage of others, or let them take advantage of you. If you are fair in your approach, then conflicts do not arise.

What was the last vocational or professional course you took, and did it help you?

Several years ago, I went to the Administrative Staff College of India (ASCI) for a course on Finance for non-Finance managers. I found it very useful. There was a course on conflict resolution that was very clear and very useful. There was yet another course on transaction analysis, which, too, I liked a lot. I haven't done any other course since then.

Do you have a connection with your hometown/place of birth/ community?

I belong to Jammu, which is a Union Territory now. My wife does a very good job of keeping in touch with everyone. Due to this, we get to visit there for family gatherings and ceremonies. Although I belong to Jammu, I got my education in UP and Jharkhand.

What is the best form of giving back to the society you have experienced and would advocate for others?

Undoubtedly education. I do a lot of charity in the health and education sectors and really enjoy it.

What is the legacy you wish to leave behind?

The company is the legacy, and I want it to be a sustained organization beyond me.

How do you define happiness? How often do you find yourself in this state?

Most forms of happiness imply that if you are not unhappy, then you are happy. But true and lasting happiness comes only when you reach God.

Any lesser-known facts about you that surprise people?

That I love photographing sunsets. There is tremendous variety in photographing sunsets.

What does spirituality mean to you, and how does it influence your approach to life?

Spirituality is about how you will attain happiness. Life's objective is to ultimately get there.

What role has education played in preparing you for the role you are now performing?

Education gives you a platform to think, analyse and understand. But what you read in a book and experience, in reality, are very different. Education plays little role in a larger life, maybe 15-20%. Education enables me to separate the chaff from grains. The rest is learning on the job. Experience is the best teacher of life.

Do you believe in discipline and routines, or are you a spontaneous person?

To me, discipline and spontaneity are not exclusive to each other. They aren't contradictory, so I believe in both. Mental makeup and how fast you can take a decision is spontaneity. The discipline of mind and work ethics are necessary to see you through to achieve your goals. Thus, both have their respective importance.

Aerospace and Defence industry

Soaring high

Foundation years

Formed in 1958, the Defence Research and Development Organization, known popularly as DRDO, is the premier government agency for the research and development of defence technologies. It is the largest defence organisation in India and the most diverse, with a network of more than 50 labs across the country covering fields such as aeronautics, armaments, electronics, land combat engineering, life sciences, materials, missiles, and naval systems.

Professor Suri Bhagvantam was formerly the Vice Chancellor of Osmania University and ex-Director of IISC, Bangalore. After his stint at IISC, he was appointed as scientific advisor to the Government of India under the Ministry of Defence. When it was decided that DRDO would be decentralised, Prof Bhagvantam recommended Hyderabad as a destination of choice. The city was considered a safe choice since it was away from the borders and thus a good place to begin a few labs. In 1962, some of the labs and their respective scientists were moved to Hyderabad. This is truly the beginning of Hyderabad's tryst with the defence sector.

The DRDL, which moved to Hyderabad in 1962, shot up to national fame with its significant contributions to the development of state-of-the-art missile systems that are deployed underwater, on sea, land as well as air-based platforms. From 1982 onwards, DRDL took a quantum jump by taking up the design and development of various types of missiles systems simultaneously and leading them to limited series production under the Integrated Guided Missiles Development Programme (IGMDP), established by the Missile Man of India, ex-president of India, Dr A.P.J. Abdul Kalam. While the

Mettle

ISRO, where Dr Kalam worked previously, focused on the launch of satellites into space, DRDL was focused on missiles for defence applications. Today DRDL, along with the other Missile Complex Laboratories, is the pioneer Missile Research laboratory in the country and Hyderabad's prized pearl.

The DMRL lab came up in 1963 and spawned the development of other nationally important technology and production centres. Mishra Dhatu Nigam (Midhani), a quasi-government enterprise, Non-Ferrous Technology Development Centre (NFTDC), and International Advanced Research Centre for Powder Metallurgy and New Materials (ARCI), all of which play an advanced role in metals and metallurgy, are based out of Hyderabad.

In 1970, Bharat Dynamics Ltd. (BDL) was founded in Hyderabad, as a PSU under the Ministry of Defence, as a manufacturing base for guided missile systems and allied equipment for the armed forces. The IGMDP has given further impetus, and BDL continues to be one of the leading manufacturers of missile equipment in the world.

Hyderabad now has seven DRDO labs and a centre of excellence. The ASL and RCI labs started by Dr Kalam are credited with pioneering research in missile technology.

Laboratory Name	Area of Research
Advanced Numerical Research & Analysis Group (ANURAG)	Computational System
Advanced Systems Laboratory (ASL)	Missiles & Strategic Systems
Centre for High Energy Systems and Sciences (CHESS)	High Energy Weapons
Defence Electronics Research Laboratory (DERL)	Electronic Warfare
Defence Metallurgical Research Laboratory (DMRL)	Metallurgy
Defence Research & Development Laboratory (DRDL)	Missile & Strategic Systems
Research Centre Imarat (RCI)	Missile & Strategic Systems

The Ordnance Factory and manufacturing segment

In the 1980s, the Govt. of India's Ministry of Defence set up 41 ordnance factories as an initiative to be the largest industrial set-up. The ordnance factories form an integrated base for indigenous production of defence hardware and equipment, with the primary objective of self-reliance in equipping the armed forces with state-of-the-art battlefield equipment. In 2021, the ordnance factories were converted into seven defence PSUs.

In 1984, the Ordnance Factory at Medak was established in Hyderabad, with the primary aim of manufacturing Infantry Combat Vehicles, the most significant being the SARATH, made for the Indian Army. The factory has continuously upgraded its facilities, evolved over the past decades and has an accredited metallurgical laboratory under its belt.

The ordnance factories played an important role in building India and ushered in the industrial revolution. Apart from this, the establishment of training schools and the founding of research organizations such as ISRO, DRDO, BDL, BEL, BEML and SAIL also contributed to the industrial growth phase of the country.

The city witnessed the growth and innovation of several allied fields for defence manufacturing, ancillary industries and component manufacturers in Hyderabad. Today, it is home to more than 1,000 MSMEs in the precision engineering industry, groomed by the defence PSUs. Several SMEs have become part of the global aerospace/defence supply chains servicing Global Original Equipment Manufacturers (OEMs).

Aviation flies high

The aviation and aerospace sector in Telangana is flying high. Hyderabad is home to 25 large companies in the Defence and Aerospace ecosystem. In a short span of time since the formation of the state in 2014, Telangana has been able to attract large investments from US OEMs such as Lockheed Martin, Boeing, GE Aviation, Pratt and Whitney, Honeywell, Collins Aerospace, etc. A few global companies such as Airbus, Saab AB and SAIC Motor Corporation also have a presence in Hyderabad.

Mettle

Also, Hyderabad has the newly built GMR Aerospace and Industrial Park - an Aerospace & Industrial cluster at the GMR Hyderabad International Airport, to meet the growing needs of manufacturing and assembling hubs in the country. Spread across an area of over 277 acres, the park offers fully serviceable industrial lands for lease or build-to-suit development purposes, manufacturing and assembling services, fully integrated Airframe Maintenance, Repair and Overhaul (MRO) company, logistics & supply chain management services, aviation and aerospace training and engineering services.

Telangana state is a strong value proposition for this industry. It has multiple aerospace parks within/near urban living centres and offers superior infrastructure at a low cost. There is abundant availability of skilled manpower, and established A&D supply chain, a strong innovation quotient, and a research-industry nexus.

Key players

A few prominent companies in the aerospace and defence segment in Hyderabad are MTAR Technologies Ltd., Premier Explosives Ltd., Ananth Technologies Ltd, Zen Technologies, HBL Power Systems, Apollo Micro Systems and Astra Microwave.

MTAR Technologies Ltd.	Testing fuelling machine columns, hydraulic cylinders, shuttle stations, engines, ball screws and other components. Prominent clients include organizations in the civilian nuclear sector, ISRO, Bharat Dynamics Ltd., RAFAEL, various labs of DRDO, Elbit Systems etc.
Premier Explosives Ltd.	Commercial explosives and detonators, solid propellants for India's missile programs, extensive research and collaboration in high-energy materials
Zen Technologies Ltd.	Design, development and manufacture of world-class state-of-the-art simulators for weapons and defence equipment
HBL Power Systems Ltd.	Batteries for industrial and defence use, including aircraft batteries
Apollo Micro Systems Ltd.	Design, development, assembly and testing of ruggedized custom-built electronic hardware & software solutions for mission-critical applications in aerospace, defence, space and homeland security
Astra Microwave Products Ltd.	Design and manufacture of sub-systems for radio frequency and microwave systems used in defence, space, meteorology and communication

Policy, Innovation and State Government thrust in the industry

A lot is happening in the field of policy and innovation, creating opportunities to further the interest in this industry.

T-Hub, India's largest technology incubator, is a state government initiative. T-Hub has partnered with leading US OEMs such as Boeing, Pratt and Whitney, Collins Aerospace, etc., to promote and accelerate start-ups in the aerospace and defence domain.

Also, underway is the state project T-Works, India's largest prototyping centre for electronics, electromechanical and mechanical start-ups. With cutting-edge infrastructure and spread over 250,000 ft, T-Works can facilitate more home-grown aerospace and defence hardware start-ups.

The state government has launched the Research and Innovation Circle of Hyderabad (RICH) to bring the research work from top scientific research institutions to market, with a special focus on aerospace and defence. To make world-class skilling accessible at affordable rates, the state government has partnered with global institutions such as Embry Riddle Aeronautical University (US), Cranfield University (UK) and Aerocampus Aquitaine (France), which offer need-based aerospace and defence certification courses in Hyderabad at relatively affordable rates.

Training support for new industries is also provided through the state-run skilling agency – Telangana Academy of Skill and Knowledge (TASK). The government is also planning to establish a world-class Aerospace University in Telangana shortly.

Mettle

DID YOU KNOW?

Hyderabad houses several prominent Public Sector Undertakings

The presence of numerous PSUs is a major thrust for the development of MSME players within the segment. Especially during the industrial revolution phase, the establishment and growth of these PSUs was a major driving force in fostering the industry, attracting and nurturing talent and spawning private entrepreneurship. In fact, some localities have been named after these large PSUs that employed thousands of people and created an ecosystem for their families to thrive. In recent decades, quite a few of the PSUs have turned sick, and both the central and state governments have started divesting stakes in some of them. Such privatization hopefully helps these organisations revive operations and turn profitable with efforts.

Some of the well-known names are:

Name of PSU	Core Business Activity
Bharat Dynamics Ltd. (BDL)	Manufacture of ammunition, guided missile systems and allied equipment for the Indian Armed Forces
Bharat Heavy Electricals Ltd.	Engineering and manufacturing company engaged in the design, engineering, construction, testing, commissioning and servicing to service power, renewable and transportation sectors, among others.
Electronics Corporation of India Ltd. (ECIL)	Established to make India build strong indigenous capability in professional grade electronics. Design, Development, Manufacture and Marketing of several products with an emphasis on three technology lines, viz. Computers, Control Systems and Communications
Hindustan Fluorocarbons Ltd.	Manufacture Poly Tetra Fluoro Ethylene (PTFE) and Chloro DI Fluoro Methane. PTFE is extensively used in chemical, mechanical, electrical and electronic industries and has strategic applications in the defence and aerospace sectors

Name of PSU	Core Business Activity
HMT Bearings Ltd.	The only company in the public sector manufacturing ball & roller bearings
Indian Drugs and Pharmaceuticals Ltd.	Bulk drug manufacturing and research for drug discovery. While these were stopped in 1996 (bulk) and 2003 (formulations), an effluent treatment plant is currently being operated.
Mishra Dhatu Nigam Ltd.	Specialized metal and metal alloys manufacturing, primarily for defence
National Mineral Development Corporation Ltd.	Exploration and production of minerals like iron ore, copper, rock phosphate, limestone, dolomite, gypsum, bentonite, magnesite, diamond, tin, tungsten, graphite, etc.
Nuclear Fuel Complex	The nuclear plant also specialises in the supply of nuclear fuel bundles and reactor core components. It is a unique facility where natural and enriched uranium fuel, zirconium alloy cladding and reactor core components are manufactured under one roof.
Ordnance Factory	Indigenous production of infantry combat vehicles. Also producing bulletproof vehicles, hulls and turrets for the main battle tank, rocket launchers, etc.

PART - V

The Tourism Industry

Editor's Note on The Tourism Industry

Hyderabad is now my home. It is not where I was born and brought up, but rather the city where I did my college and professional education. I have spent about two decades now in Hyderabad. During my years at college and early years at work, I happened to explore the geography of the city-taking public buses on my two-wheeler or catching rides with colleagues on their bikes. I have visited some of the tourist spots mentioned in the following section with my family, friends, extended family and colleagues. But I must say that when I was writing this, I was mesmerised by the facts and details I discovered. The intricacies of architecture, the stories behind why and how some of the monuments were conceptualised and constructed, and the claim to fame of some of the attractions -all made for a very interesting find.

Tourism, it seems, is always for visitors. I once read somewhere that you must play tourist in your own city. That is so true. I realised that I have not taken my kids to see the Salar Jung museum or Golconda fort in Hyderabad but have taken them to forts in other cities of India.

Hyderabad is definitely an exciting and enticing tourist destination. I have attempted to categorize the places to visit and attractions and can easily see how there is something for everyone. Art, food, architecture, history, contemporary theatre and art, nature and birding, old-world charm and modernity, and affordable, mid-range and upscale dining experiences, to name a few. I was filled with a sense of pride and wonder as I put this all together. The Telangana government has a wonderful website dedicated to tourism both in Hyderabad as well as other major districts.

If you haven't been a tourist in Hyderabad, I beckon you to be one now.

A Tourist Hub

The City of Nizams

Hyderabad is known as the *City of Nizams*. The Nizams ruled from 1724 to 1948, when the State became a part of the Union of India. The Nizams were among the wealthiest people in the world, and their patronage of art, literature, food and culture shaped Hyderabad over the two centuries they ruled. The city is known for many things, such as the Charminar monument, biryani, high-quality pearls and lac bangles, but these are just a few things that make her special. She has so much to offer to the spiritual, the food aficionados, nature lovers, animal lovers, and those interested in art, literature, architecture and history. More recently, due to an explosion of multinational organisations, there is a mixed ethnic diversity in the city, and it has plenty of options for those looking for trendy cafes, watering holes and discotheques. Hyderabad is the fourth largest city in India, with a population of more than seven million, and rated one of the best places to live in the country. As a tourist destination, there is so much to see, and with the efforts of the Telangana tourism department, it is sure to gain more visitors and popularity.

For the religious

Some of the most popular tourist destinations are places of worship. The craftsmanship and styles are so varied, and there is something for people of each faith to pay a visit to when touring the city.

The Birla Temple

Constructed in 1976 on a 280 feet high hillock off the southern side of the Hussain Sagar Lake is the white marble temple known as the

Birla Mandir. It is a blend of various architectural styles Dravidian, Rajasthani and Utkala. The sanctum sanctorum is 42 feet high and has a replica of the Tirumala temple Venkateswara. It is primarily a Venkateswara temple but has separate shrines for other Gods such as Shiva, Ganesh, Saraswati, Hanuman, Brahma, Lakshmi and Saibaba. It also has a separate temple dedicated to Buddha.

Hyderabad Then and Now

Durgam Cheruvu   Durgam Cheruvu

The Jagannath Temple

Modelled along the Puri Jagannath Temple in Orissa is the spacious Jagannath Temple in Banjara Hills. Constructed in 3,000 square yards, it is a smaller scaled version of the Puri temple. It has a 70-feet high striking peak, and the signature red sandstone used in its construction was brought in from Orissa. The temple has gained much popularity in recent years and has several small shrines apart from the sanctum sanctorum that houses the Jagannath idol with Balabhadra and Subhadra. The temple is quite famous for its '*rath yatra,*' or chariot festival, when the main idols are decorated and taken on chariots to bless devotees irrespective of caste, creed and race.

Peddamma Temple

The Peddamma Temple is an important landmark in Jubilee Hills and is approximately 150 years old. The Rajagopuram was constructed only in 1993. The Goddess or Ammavaru is very popular, and thousands of devotees come to seek her blessings. While the Telangana festival of Bonalu is celebrated once a year, at this temple, it is celebrated every Sunday.

St. Mary's Church

The St. Mary's Church, built in Indo-Gothic style architecture, is a Roman Catholic church in the heart of Secunderabad. It was sanctified in 1850. Famed for its architecture, the church has curved arches, a buttress and several side altars devoted to the saints. During Christmas, it is a visual delight with all its bright lights. People of all faiths visit the church for its architectural beauty.

Chilkur Balaji Temple

One of the oldest Balaji temples in Telangana is in Chilkur, on the banks of Osman Sagar. The temple doesn't accept any donations and does not have a hundi. It also does not have any privileged entry for VIPs. People often make a wish or take a vow and circumambulate the shrine 11 times. Once the wish is fulfilled, they return and circumambulate 108 times.

In recent decades, it gained popularity as the 'Visa God'. A lot of people who apply for visas to the US offer prayers at this temple and go back with gratitude once their visas are granted.

Makkah Masjid

Overlooking the famed Charminar is the Makkah Masjid, built by the Qutb Shahi rulers. The central arch of the mosque is made of bricks made of the soil brought from Makkah, thus giving it the name Makkah Masjid. It is one of India's finest mosques, a marvel in size and a prized creation with intricate design work. The prayer hall can accommodate more than 10,000 people. The interiors of the mosque are opulent with royal carpets, Belgian crystal chandeliers, and writings from the Quran in gold thread.

For the love of art and architecture

The Qutb Shahi dynasty ruled Hyderabad from 1518 A.D. to 1687 A.D. and was the dynasty to rule before the city was absorbed by the Mughal empire. The Charminar, The Golconda Fort and the Qutb Shahi tombs are fine examples of architecture of the period and form the most popular and iconic monumental representations of Hyderabad. The Golconda Fort is a fortified citadel from where the royal family reigned, and it consists of military structures, pavilions, religious structures, landscaped gardens and water systems. The Charminar is a symbolic fulcrum in the city; its four gateways facing four cardinal directions served to plan the city. The Qutb Shahi tombs are a royal necropolis consisting of tombs, mosques and -a mortuary bath. Together, the three monuments are a testament to the Qutb Shahi dynasty and their skilled, innovative architecture.

Charminar

The Charminar is the most iconic mosque, a symbol of Hyderabad. It literally means four minarets' or towers. The Charminar is at the heart of Hyderabad's Old City. It was built by the Qutb Shahi rulers to commemorate the end of a deadly plague in 1591. Located close to the banks of the Musi river, the monument is made in Indo-Islamic architectural style, with Persian elements. The delicate floral design, stucco decorations, balustrades and balconies make for a masterpiece. Each minaret has 149 circular steps leading to the top. It also houses a mosque where prayers can be offered. The four clocks were added in the year 1889. The area around Charminar is very busy, and close by is the famous Laad bazaar or Chudi bazaar, where one can buy lac bangles. When illuminated at night, the Charminar is a sight to take in and hugely popular with locals as much as with tourists. In 2019, it averaged more than a lakh visitors each month.

Charminar

Golconda Fort

The western part of Hyderabad has the majestic and magnificent Golconda Fort, which got its name from the Telugu words 'Golla Konda,' meaning Shepherd's Hill.

Golconda Fort

Mettle

Built by the Kakatiya rulers in the 13th century as a small mud fort around an idol, it was extended into a full-fledged fortress by the Qutb Shahi rulers and eventually conquered by Aurangzeb who intentionally left it in ruins.

One of the city's iconic landmarks, this fort rests on a granite hill 120 metres high and has a perimeter of about 11 km. It is a collection of palaces, mosques and pavilions, drawbridges, cannons, majestic halls and stables. The outermost entrance is known as the *Fateh Darwaza* or Victory Gate. The fort is famed for its acoustical excellence - a handclap made at the entrance is audible at the top of the pavilion, about 1 km away. This design served as a warning system to alert members of the royal family of any impending dangers. The evening sound and light show at the fort is very popular, with commentary by legendary actor Amitabh Bachchan.

Qutb Shahi tombs

The Quli Qutb Shahi tombs are yet another architectural marvel in the city. They were constructed in the 1500s as a place of rest for the afterlife of the rulers. The 106 acres of sprawling land consists of 23 mosques, five wells and 40 mausoleums. The architecture is intricate in style, and the place is replete with scriptures, archways, parapets and domed structures. The lush day and night gardens and the Turkish mortuary bath are a testament to the careful planning that went into constructing these tombs. The tombs are being restored by the Aga Khan Trust.

Salar Jung Museum

One of Hyderabad's most famous tourist spots is the Salar Jung Museum, famous across the world for having the largest one-man collection of antiques. Nawab Mir Yusuf Ali Khan Salar Jung III, the former Prime minister of the 7th Nizam of Hyderabad, spent most of his savings on collecting priceless

Salar Jung Museum

artefacts from all over the world. The museum boasts a collection of 43,000 art objects, 50,000 books and manuscripts showcased in 38 galleries on two floors.

The collections range from Indian Art, Middle Eastern Art, European Art, Far Eastern Art, Children's Art, etc. It also houses the world-famous statue of Veiled Rebecca and Marguerite and Mephistopheles, a fine collection of jade and daggers owned by Queen Noor Jahan, Emperors Shah Jahan, Aurangzeb's sword and other timeless masterpieces.

Adventure and more sight-seeing

The Hussain Sagar Lake and Buddha Statue

Hyderabad and Secunderabad are twin cities, separated by the man-made Hussain Sagar Lake. The lake is historically significant as the treaty between the Mughals and Golconda was settled on its banks. This subsequently began to be known as 'Bund' in the 1990s, which means dam, and the area came to be known as the Tank Bund. At the centre of the heart-shaped lake is the majestic monolithic Gautam Buddha statue. It is said that the former Chief Minister of Andhra Pradesh, Mr N.T. Rama Rao was inspired by the Statue of Liberty during his visit to the US in 1984 and, with a desire to bring something similar to Hyderabad, chose the Buddha statue. Sunsets at the Tank Bund with the Buddha statue form a picturesque, photo-worthy scene.

Salar Jung Museum

Attractions such as the NTR Park, Lumbini Park, Hussain Sagar Lake, Jalavihar and Necklace Road, all within a two km radius, make the area very popular for locals and tourists.

Lumbini Park

Ramoji Film City

The Ramoji Film City is an immensely popular tourist attraction, certified by Guinness World Records as the largest film studio complex. It is a thematic holiday destination spread over 1600 acres and has movie sets, hotels, restaurants, adventure activities, thematic gardens and fountains, amusement parks, a bird park, butterfly park and several other activities for families. The film city tour is extremely popular, where you get to see permanent sets as well as temporary ones. The guided tour takes you through famous movie sets and describes popular film shoots that have taken place in the film city. About 1.5 million visitors visit this place annually. The star hotels and attractive tourist packages, bus rides and inside tours make for a major attraction for people from across the country and abroad.

Ramoji Film City

DID YOU KNOW?

Tollywood, the Telugu film industry, has many entries in the Guinness Book of World Records.

- The Ramoji Film City is the largest film studio complex in the world
- D. Rama Naidu is the most prolific producer
- Dasari Narayana Rao for the most directed films
- Brahmanandam for acting in the most single-language films
- Vijaya Nirmala is the female director with most films

Tollywood films entertain the masses and have a very large audience in both domestic and overseas markets. In fact, 'Film Nagar in the western part of the city is considered the headquarters for Tollywood, as it is home to several tinsel town stars as well as production houses. Annapurna Studios, set up by late actor Akkineni Nagewara Rao and Ramanaidu Studio, set up by late producer D. Ramanaidu are two very large, old and iconic studios of Hyderabad.

Themed Parks

Themed parks such as Ocean Park, Wonderla, Snow World and other adventure camps cum recreational parks are popular among youth. Several resorts offer adventure sports within the facilities or in the vicinity, and activities such as zip lining, rock climbing, coracle rides, boating, jumping, etc., can be explored.

For nature lovers and bird watchers, there are several forest areas, lakes and reservoirs around the city and its outskirts, and groups of people can be found taking advantage of this in the early hours on weekends and holidays. Manjeera Bird Sanctuary, Osman Sagar, Ananthagiri forest, Ameenpur lake and Narsapur forest are some of the birding hotspots close to the city.

Food, culture, shopping

Food

The biryani of Hyderabad is world famous. Popular biryani chains in Hyderabad are Paradise, Shah Ghouse, Pista House and Sarvi, to name a few. But, aside from biryani, Hyderabad has a plethora of mouth-watering Telugu cuisines. The spicy *avakaya* pickle and a surfeit of tangy and spicy chutneys popularly known as *pachadis*, fiery Andhra and Rayalaseema non-vegetarian preparations, and savouries of Telangana make for a delectable range that caters to every foodie.

Hyderabad is also a famous culinary tourist destination. Treats that appease the sweet tooth, such as *Double ka meetha, Gajar ka halwa, Kubani ka meetha, Badam ki Jhab* (marzipan), and *Dil-e-Firdaus* are uniquely Hyderabadi.

As one of the leading cosmopolitan cities in South India with a blend of Indian ethnic populace, Hyderabad is home to various restaurants and food outlets serving different Indian native cuisines from South to North and East to West. In addition, several Continental, American and Middle Eastern offerings have also come up in the recent decade, and it can easily be said that Hyderabad accommodates every palate.

Shopping

Hyderabad has the moniker City of Pearls, and truly pearls are something everyone can shop for in Hyderabad. The Nizams proudly wore their pearls, and due to the heavy influence of Persian culture, the city gained prominence in the trading of pearls. While the Pathargatti and Charminar areas in Old City are famous for pearls, some of the larger pearl and jewellery traders have established stores all over town.

Shilparamam

A shopping trip is incomplete without a visit to Shilparamam and Charminar. Shilparamam is an ethnic village at the heart of Hi-tech City, the newer part of town. The village, spread over 65 acres, has handlooms and arts and crafts on display from all over the country. There are also two museums, an open-air amphitheatre and recreational activities within the complex. Cultural festivals, dance and music performances and concerts of both the free and paid variety are regularly held to promote Indian art and culture. With a vast range of products for sale, there is something that fits every budget in Shilparamam. It is indeed rare for anyone to return empty-handed from this place.

The Charminar shopping area is also well known, particularly for pearls, fabrics, dresses, jewellery and trinkets, as well as the lac bangles in the famed Chudi Bazaar. With a big export market in the Middle East and an attraction for locals and tourists alike, the Charminar shops offer a unique experience. The streets of Charminar are filled with bustle, with pedestrians, street vendors and tiny shops dotting all the roads around the area. During important festivals such as Eid, the place comes fully alive and is thronged by crowds of avid shoppers.

A hallmark Hyderabadi experience is incomplete without a visit to the annual consumer exhibition 'Numaish'. Located in Nampally, the vast exhibition ground spread over 23 acres hosts a massive exhibition of handicrafts, goods and wares from all over India. The exhibition completed 80 years of existence and recently received a trademark license. Food, games and joyrides ensure that every family member has something to cherish at the exhibition. Perhaps, barring the current generation of mall-goers, city folk attend this annual fair with pride and enthusiasm.

Apart from this, Hyderabad has several multiplexes, malls, standalone shops and nationally reputed chains of apparel, footwear, jewellery and lifestyle stores. Luxury brands and city designers entice consumers with advertisements and attractive window displays. Hyderabad can easily be called a haven for shoppers.

Culture

The Ravindra Bharati Auditorium, Shilpakala Vedika Auditorium, Harihara Kala Bhavan and Gachibowli stadium are some of the large indoor and outdoor venues where performances and concerts are held. The city has a healthy appetite for various dance forms, music, theatre and concerts. Movies in multiplexes, flea markets like the Sol Sante, beer fests, theatre and stand-up comedy, and a host of new forms of entertainment are gaining popularity in recent times.

The HITEX Exhibition Centre is one of India's largest exhibition complexes and home to many national and international conferences, expos, fetes and exhibitions across various industries and genres. The facilities were constructed to international standards in consultation with the globally acclaimed Messe Dusseldorf, a world leader in trade fairs and exhibitions.

Parks and recreational centres

Hyderabad has several parks where walkers, runners, bikers, athletes, and kids can work out outdoors or spend time leisurely with their families. Sanjeevaiah Park, Jalagam Vengal Rao Park, Anjaiah Lumbini Park, Indira Park, Krishna Kant Park, Public Gardens, Necklace Road, Hyderabad Central University area,

Mettle

Kasu Brahmananda Reddy Park and Botanical Gardens are some of the prominent ones. Popular annual athletic events such as the Airtel Marathon, Devil's Circuit and Brevets de Randonneurs are commonly conducted in the city. The Lal Bahadur Shastri stadium at Nampally and the Gachibowli stadium at Gachibowli host some of the big sporting and entertainment events in the city.

PART - VI

The Services Sector

Editor's Note on the Services Sector

In 1978, the State of Andhra Pradesh established the Society for Employment Promotion & Training in Twin Cities (SETWIN) to create employment opportunities and provide training for the city's unemployed. The jobs were all in the services sector. SETWIN provides training in computers, management, spoken English, technicians and media profiles. Over decades, SETWIN helped a few lakh individuals in getting employed and generating income for their families. The services sector, at that time, was a minuscule one compared to where we are today.

The one sector that has seen exponential growth in a short span of time, with a wide-reaching impact on several other industries, is the knowledge sector. Services, with a capability to address the needs of large export markets such as Europe and the Americas, created enormous wealth for the city and its residents.

Cut to the year 2000-the, Hi-tech City 'Cyber Towers' building stood amidst brown dirt roads. The next milestone building was the Wipro one, followed by the Vanenburg IT Parks, a few km down the road. The rest was empty space, waiting for buildings to spring up. Initial occupants would remember how difficult it was to get public transport to this 'remote' area. There was no metro or many buses that would ply in this area, and autorickshaw drivers would be reluctant to drop customers without assurance of a return ride.

Cut to 2020 and beyond, and you will see how in two decades, the area is exploding with activity. Numerous commercial buildings, residential gated communities, eateries, entertainment zones and malls dot the landscape. Several global organisations of repute have built offices here. To name a few - Deloitte, Microsoft, Google, Facebook, Amazon, Dell, Hewlett Packard, ADP, Oracle, Samsung and Motorola - all established large R&D centres in Hyderabad. Indigenous large tech companies such as TCS, Infosys, Tech Mahindra and Cognizant also employ thousands of people and have large campuses in the city.

The technology revolution created several billionaire enterprises and people in Hyderabad and currently employs about 6,00,000 people across 1,500 companies. The export revenues of this industry are close to $15bn, the second largest in the country after Bangalore.

Thousands of people from Andhra Pradesh and Telangana migrated overseas and took up jobs in other countries. It is no wonder that Hyderabad got the US embassy to open a local visa processing centre to handle large volumes and high demand, previously serviced at Chennai for all of South India. Foreign exchequers and money remittances to India saw an exponential rise, and suddenly, middle-class families started having an easy flow of money. Several families saw children earning salaries much higher than what their parents earned at retirement.

The ancillary growth created by the tech revolution brought even more enterprises and generated income for several lakhs of individuals. Transportation, food, retail and groceries, apparel, schooling, entertainment, residential, and commercial buildings -all sprung up to support the people working in this industry. The areas of Madhapur, Kondapur, Gachibowli and the Financial District have flourished in the last two decades, so much so that NRIs are surprised at each visit to this part of the city, with its ever-changing landscape.

The following section describes the riveting rise of the service sector in the city, led from the front by the IT& ITES industry. Also profiled in this section are interviews of two entrepreneurs from the city. The first is a man who played a key role in the city's IT evolution. It took a lot of effort to bring the first few multinational companies to Hyderabad, and the exponential growth happened after critical mass was attained. The journey from Hyderabad to Cyberabad is

Mettle

remarkable and transformational for the city, one that puts it firmly on the global map. The second entrepreneur is a lady who went against all norms and family conventions to get educated and subsequently joined her husband in running a business enterprise. A woman who inspires by her words and her actions and stands for women's rights to education, dignity and independence. Meeting and interviewing these very accomplished and talented entrepreneurs has been a wonderful experience for me, and I expect you will feel the same way when you read about them.

J A Chowdary

Chairman
Indian Blockchain Standards Committee
Founding member, SucSeed Indovation Fund
Co-founder and Executive Chairman of Talent Sprint 2010-2015
Managing Director NVIDIA Graphics 2006-2009
President & CEO, Co-founder, Portal Player 1999-2006
Founding Director of STPI Bangalore, Hyderabad, Chennai

J.A. Chowdary is a first-generation entrepreneur hailing from a small village in the Anantapur district. He witnessed a phenomenal career transformation that began as a college teacher, then as a scientist at ISRO and then went on to be a bureaucrat with the Government of India. After this, he became a technocrat, entrepreneur, and eventually a serial investor and mentor. With a double Masters's from IIT Madras & SK University, he played a key role in the IT transformation journey of Hyderabad as the founding director of Software Technology Parks of India (STPI), Bangalore, Hyderabad & Chennai. J.A. Chowdary made a very significant & long-lasting contribution in the formative years of the 'Hyderabad to Cyberabad' journey. He subsequently co-founded two companies over the years - Portal Player and Talent Sprint. He now continues to invest in and mentor several tech startups and is passionate about providing healthy organic food through his organic farms in his village.

INTERVIEW

I knocked at the gate of Hill Ridge Villas, where Mr J.A. Chowdary was in conversation with a professional colleague over a cup of coffee. I did not want to interrupt them, but he got up and waved me in. I said I could come back, but he assured me no big secrets were being discussed and immediately made me feel warm and welcome. After a cup of coffee and basic introductions, I proceeded with the interview in the comfort of his living room. He warned me that his answers would be long, story-like and that I would have to derive my answers from them. I gladly accepted. I also mentioned that I do not need to record conversations as I can type fast and store the rest in my memory, and he quickly gave an anecdote of how Tenali Raman once threw a challenge to a scribe in the court of Krishnadevaraya, making it impossible for him to transcribe a particular conversation. I laughed and said I would still try. With this warm-hearted ice-breaker, we started our long conversations that ran into a two-part interview, which left me with a complete picture of the thoughts, events and inner workings of the mind of the very accomplished Mr J.A. Chowdary, who was extremely down-to-earth, honest and open with me.

So what is it that makes you spring out of bed each morning?

I have lived a fortunate life where I do things that matter and make me feel good. Being involved in projects that are close to my heart and spending time with my precious grandchildren and other family members make me spring out of bed every day.

What do you believe is the purpose of your life, personally?

I believe in simplicity; whatever God pushes me to do, I try to do my best in it. With God's grace, I have been able to fulfil some of those aspirations.

At what age do you think you identified this, and what were your motivating factors?

It is difficult to pinpoint a specific age when I discovered my purpose. However, I did not have confidence in my early childhood and experienced some lows in the early part of my career. Over the course of my life, after having shaped the IT space at Hyderabad and successfully founded Portal Player and Talent Sprint, I could connect with people, harness my strengths and do well. This kept me going.

Who or what has been the greatest influence in your life? A person, a book, a saying or a transformational moment you'd like to describe?

There are three people who greatly influenced my life.

First is my mother, who always encouraged me, despite me being a poor student at school and fading compared to my sister, who was excellent at everything.

Second is my fourth standard teacher Mr Anjanappa, who was the first person who infused confidence in me that I could do something in life. He took an innovative approach to teach through poems, drama, and enactment and helped me discover my love for performing on stage. I won a local poetry recital contest, which instilled a lot of confidence in me. It was truly a turning point in my life.

The third person who inspired me a lot was Dr A.P.J. Abdul Kalam. Although I met him through my first job at ISRO, Bangalore, it was during his stint at DRDO that I interacted with him. I was helping out with the Lead India initiative, which he founded. The best thing about Dr Kalam is how down-to-earth he was, how he used to inspire and speak to the youth and motivate them, and finally, how he left this world addressing a big group of children. I am trying to follow in his footsteps.

They say the morning habits set a person's day up for success and productivity. What's the morning routine like before you get to work?

My morning routines are a little different depending on where I am. Since the onset of COVID, I have spent a lot of time in my village and at my daughter's house.

When at my daughter's house, I wake up at 04:00 am and start planning my day while still in bed and am careful not to wake anyone up. Next, I take a walk indoors, do some basic stretching, and on some days, I meditate for 15-20 mins. Once my grandkids wake up, I play with them, water plants and make them do *Suryanamaskars* to salute the living God. I then read motivational messages on WhatsApp, listen to Ted Talks, and share them if I really like them. This is my routine before getting to work.

When I am in my village, I wake up early and join my brother in the morning prayers. I do *Suryanamaskars* and *Tulsipradakshanas* and walk around our land. I spend some time with my aged mother and then sit down to a hearty, healthy, millet-based breakfast before getting onto work.

What was the last most interesting book you read and why? Which book do you think everyone must read and why?

My family comprises many readers; however, I am not one of them. I have a funny anecdote about this. When I co-founded Portal Player, we had a consultant who worked with all four of us founders to identify our personalities and bring out synergies. He spent a day with each founder. When he gave me my assessment, he said I am good with people and strategy, but on the negative side, I don't read and am not detail-oriented. I said I would try to improve, but he said it is my genetic make-up and that I cannot change, and he was quite insistent about it! He said I need a good executive assistant to summarise things for me. I tend to believe him because it is still true that I cannot read anything long and wordy. So, to sum up, I don't have a favourite book or a recommendation.

What hobbies do you pursue currently, and how often do you find time for them?

My hobby is to enable people, mobilise people and bring about change in society and community. From time to time, I take up passion projects with a high impact on society.

Currently, I am working on two projects: one to change how our children learn and the second to change the quality of food we consume nowadays. Both of these make a big impact and are close to my heart.

I once ran a Let's Vote campaign to educate the educated on the importance and responsibility of citizens in electing their government. It is important for professional employees also to participate in the process of democracy by exercising their vote for electing the right leadership.

For all the projects I enjoy, I was always able to find enough time–some of the highlights have been Let's Vote, College Connect, Vikasa Bharathi, etc. Additionally, I've also aided in setting up institutions such as HYSEA, American Chamber of Commerce, TiE Hyderabad, Food 360 Foundation, etc.

What do you think is the biggest lesson you learnt in 2020, the year of COVID?

I think as a nation, we were just not prepared for a pandemic. The second wave showed gaping holes in awareness and seriousness about COVID. And we lost many lives because of this, many businesses suffered, and breadwinners were taken away. I think responsible citizens should have planned and managed the situation better to save the lives of many individuals and families.

On the positive side, family values have taken priority during and due to the pandemic. Many people returned to their villages and cities to care for and spend time with their parents. In the service industry, erstwhile excuses for not allowing remote working quickly evaporated, and many are able to work from home now, managing both work and household responsibilities to their best abilities. The rural economy is now on the rise, and the gap between urban and rural growth has reduced. The situation also gave a chance to leaders, policymakers and citizens to think about the fact that the Gandhian way of building vibrant rural economies could be realised.

At a higher level, I think nature has always shown human beings their place. There have been depressions, wars and pandemics before. There's a good and bad side to everything. The COVID pandemic showed the vulnerability of human beings and that all are equal when it comes to natural calamities of this proportion.

What's your favourite quote of all time?

The Nike slogan with a tick mark–Just Do It. I always tell people to get into execution; whatever you want to do, just do it. Get into the action, whatever you believe is right.

What do you tell yourself when you face insurmountable challenges? Typically, things where you need to make tough decisions?

Big risks and challenges are a part of life. I accept them as part of life. Once you dive into the water, you have to swim, right? I take the ups and downs in my stride and use my strengths to keep moving forward in life. During difficult times, we usually get innovative ideas which are useful in life. Every problem gives an opportunity to think and innovate for an entrepreneur. These things are balanced by the Almighty to push growth and innovation through opportunities.

Just as Krishna lifted a mountain to protect his fellow beings, an entrepreneur who does his bit can generate employment and lift up the livelihood of thousands of fellow humans.

Do you feel stressed and overwhelmed? What do you do to cope with stress?

Definitely, I have been through immensely stressful situations-financial stress, health stress, and work-related pressures. I have overcome so many of these, and I have a strong belief that God has helped me in my most troubled times. I try not to get scared of anything. I have the 'Gabbar Singh' philosophy -*'Jo darrgaya, woh mar gaya'*. The stressful situations pass, and life is always restored to normalcy. Since I have experienced it so many times, I know these situations will come and go. Life continues always.

What is the single piece of advice you would like to give your peers?

First, fulfil your family responsibilities and ensure they are taken care of. First, win the war at home. Bring stability, tranquillity and happiness to the people depending on you. Then you can conquer the world; using your abilities, talent and skills, you can innovate or start something and help the larger society. Bring peace within, peace around you and then bring it everywhere.

Have you thought about how you'd spend your time after retirement?

I feel there is no retirement for anyone. Until the body permits, the mind and body should be kept active. All knowledge acquired should be shared. I don't advise anyone to think that I am retired. In fact, I prefer that this word be removed from the dictionary.

People should always keep doing something. There are many opportunities, such as working with youth, students and communities. One must try to create a happy, positive ecosystem wherever they are. There is a company in Hong Kong working on the concept of 'Retired But Ready' to engage the services of retired people to serve organizations and societies.

How do you measure yourself? Do you have quantitative or qualitative goals that you track and measure yourself against?

I do not have grand visions and checklists. I think, so far in life, I was guided by God and went and delivered in whichever direction I was pushed. Goals, planning and checklists don't really work for me. I have impulsive thoughts, and then I follow up on them and continuously execute them. Each day, I utilise the day and make the most of it. That is all I measure now - giving my best each day.

What are a couple of words your family would use to describe you?

A He-Man, and a forever young at heart person who always does above and beyond for the community and society

What is the one piece of advice you'd give your children?

Do whatever you want to, and I will support you. Be positive, and don't look at things through a negative lens. Don't criticize and complain. Do your best with the resources and circumstances you have, as there are always immense possibilities.

How do you approach difficult conversations and conflicts? Could you share what has worked for you?

I have been through many conflicts, troubled and even humiliating times. I think the only approach I can share is my faith in God. He has seen me through all the difficult situations. I believe in cosmic energy. For everyone, a strong belief system is important -whether in self, energy, a God, or whatever it may be, a belief system will see you through most conflicts and situations.

What was the last vocational or professional course you took, and did it help you?

I don't think I have done any specific courses that have helped me. Everything I have learned is through conversations with people and by observation. There is continuous learning from mentors, peers, and all my human interactions. I think I am in a workshop every day, learning something new. My work is a workshop that teaches me every day.

Do you have a connection with your hometown/place of birth/community?

Yes, very much. I come from a village named Battalapalli in Anantapur district, one of the most backward districts in the country. Basic amenities like water, employment from industries, etc., didn't exist throughout my childhood and early adulthood. The village was like a desert with no greenery.

Things have, however, improved now. Industries such as Kia Motors and Gerdau Steel (now Arjas) have come in and provided employment opportunities. The water table has increased, and some of the hydro water projects like Pattiseema and Handri-Neeva helped recharge the lakes and borewells. This led to an improvement in agriculture also.

Thanks to the pandemic, I don't travel much anywhere, and I have spent a lot of quality time in my village in the last two years. I am deeply connected with my village and enjoy my time there. My aged mother and brother and extended family stay there. Both as a duty and by choice, I happily spend a lot of time with my 93-year-old mother, as she is in the nirvana stage of her journey. We pray together, eat together, and I conduct my work and calls, enjoying the simple luxuries that village life has to offer. I also spend a lot of time on my organic farm, where we are doing herbal farming and growing oranges and guavas.

What is the best form of giving back to the society you have experienced and would advocate for others?

The first is *Vidya danam* - Undoubtedly, education is the best form of giving back to society.

The second is '*Udyogadanam*' - giving jobs. Entrepreneurs who are capable of doing something should, as this provides employment opportunities directly and indirectly to thousands of people and ultimately benefits an entire community.

These years, since I spend a lot of time in my village, a minimum of five people who are unemployed despite being educated seek my help every day. I remain very accessible by being in the village physically and try to help them by getting them employment and connecting them to various organisations that I know.

What is the legacy you wish to leave behind?

I do not think of legacy as such. Be good, do good and make yourself useful until you leave. That is all I believe in.

How do you define happiness? How often do you find yourself in this state?

Happiness is in doing something good. Happiness is playing with my grandchildren. Making my mom recover from her deathbed gave me happiness. Agriculture gives me happiness. Seeing my projects come to fruition gives me happiness. The success of my mentees gives me a lot of happiness.

Any lesser-known facts about you that surprise people?

My educational background surprises a lot of people. The fact that I was a mediocre student from a Telugu medium background and made it so far in life.

What does spirituality mean to you, and how does it influence your approach to life?

I am deeply spiritual in my faith. The situations, dangers and challenges that I have faced in life, I think only God has pulled me through. I am very grateful for it and pray and thank God as often as possible. All that I have achieved, overcome, and done for others in life is with His help and with Him watching over me.

What role has education played in preparing you for the role you are now performing?

Education laid the foundation for everything that I am. Although I was not the brightest student, I did MSc. and MTech, and since then, I did not look back. I worked for the government and took a leap into the private sector. Most of my career growth happened due to skills and abilities I developed rather than my degrees. However, education gets a foot in the door for many, and it is therefore important as a foundation.

Do you believe in discipline and routines, or are you a spontaneous person?

I am a completely spontaneous person. Even my speeches and presentations are extempore, be it at government programs and functions or fundraising in Silicon Valley. I have never been a 'prepared' person.

Vanitha Datla

Vice Chairperson and Managing Director, Elico Ltd.
Managing Director, Elico Healthcare Services Ltd.
www.elico.co

Vanitha Datla is a leading face of women's education, empowerment and upliftment in Hyderabad. Against odds, she pursued higher education late in life and holds a CFA and an MBA degree from the ICFAI business school in Hyderabad. Vanitha Datla joined her husband, and together they run Elico Ltd. and Elico Healthcare Services. Elico was founded by her husband, Ramesh Datla's uncle, Mr D.V.S. Raju, in 1960 with the intent to create indigenous technology and empower import substitution in the niche field of analytical instruments design, development and manufacture. The company's subsidiary, Elico Healthcare Services Ltd, is a preferred service provider to several overseas clients in the healthcare industry. Elico also strategically diversified into the ITES segment two decades ago to help de-risk and scale up. Vanitha is currently pursuing an Executive Doctoral program with the Indian School of Business and is associated with leading industry and networking forums in various capacities.

Established In	Revenue for FY 20-21	Number of employees
1960	**100** crores	**900**

Expertise

Analytical Instruments Design & Manufacturing and Healthcare Services Company

INTERVIEW

I stepped into the offices of Elico Ltd. at the appointed hour and walked up to be shown into the cabin of the elegant and effervescent Ms Vanitha. She was extremely courteous in receiving me, and after a brief introduction, we went into a wonderful conversation about 'women empowerment,' something we both have strong views on. Through the conversation, I learned of Ms Vanitha's journey, her passion for helping others and especially her focus on uplift of women. We spoke of how different upbringings impact children, especially girls, who are not encouraged enough to pursue education and careers. We spoke of how some aspects of society have changed but how much more needs to be done. It was a lively, passionate discussion, and I was amazed to learn everything that Ms Vanitha accomplished in her life, particularly with her Women in Network NGO, through which the lives of many slum children have been enriched over the past 15 years. The one-hour allocated quickly went by, and we agreed to finish the rest of the interview the next day. This being the only interview with a woman entrepreneur, I left the office feeling inspired and empowered.

So what is it that makes you spring out of bed each morning?

It isn't a conscious thing to think of every morning, but I always look forward to something exciting in the day and hope for a better situation.

What do you believe is the purpose of your life, personally?

To be able to help other people in whatever ways I can.

At what age do you think you identified this, and what were your motivating factors?

Sometime in my early twenties, I always felt I could help other people. When you can help others, it makes the environment much happier to be in.

Who or what has been the greatest influence in your life? A person, a book, a saying or a transformational moment you'd like to describe?

My grandfather and my father have been my biggest influences. I spent some time with my grandfather during my growing up years.

His passion and work ethic left a deep impact on me. My father, a devoted surgeon, also influenced me. I wanted to become a doctor like my father. He is dedicated and meticulous - two traits I definitely inherited from him.

They say the morning habits set a person's day up for success and productivity. What's the morning routine like before you get to work?

For the most part, my morning routine consists of exercise. I do a combination of running, cycling, gymming and sports. After exercise, if I don't have kitchen work, the next thing I do is get ready for work.

What was the last most interesting book you read and why?

'Becoming' by Michelle Obama. It is very admirable what Michelle did, and the book encapsulates her life, goals and beliefs beautifully.

Which book do you think everyone must read and why?

'Little Women' by Louisa May Alcott. It is a coming-of-age story of four girls and their mother, who learn to be resilient and stand on their own feet despite many challenges with an absentee father figure. I think everyone should read it to understand things from a woman's perspective.

What hobbies do you pursue currently, and how often do you find time for them?

I currently have no hobbies and no time. Most of my free time goes into preparing for my Executive Doctoral Program with the Indian School of Business, Hyderabad. Whenever I get spare time, I love spending it with my two granddaughters, the love of my life.

What do you think is the biggest lesson you learnt in 2020, the year of COVID?

Adaptability, resilience and being thick-skinned. When running a business in tough times, we are faced with so many issues, challenges, etc. It helps to be unemotional when making decisions. Whatever comes our way, we learn to take it with equanimity rather than with emotions. People think being an entrepreneur is a bed of roses, but it is not. Tough decisions and criticism are all part of the plate, and with the COVID situation, one had to be even more thick-skinned to get through the difficult times.

What's your favourite quote of all time?

A quote by the Dalai Lama, "Our prime purpose in life is to help others, and if you can't help them, at least don't hurt them."

What do you tell yourself when you face insurmountable challenges? Typically, things where you need to make tough decisions?

I try my best, given the situation and context. Internally, I am aware that this, too, shall pass. So I take things with a pinch of salt and keep my peace. The magic is to balance decision-making and take both good and bad times in life in stride.

Do you feel stressed and overwhelmed? What do you do to cope with stress?

Yes, there are times when things can get stressful and overwhelming. I look at the situation from different angles, rehash it, and then break it down into small actionable items. Addressing items one by one then helps me overcome the overwhelm.

What is the single piece of advice you would like to give your peers?

Help women when you can, and keep an eye out for women who need to come up in life. Gender parity, more women in leadership, positions of influence and decision-making are the answers to many of the world's current problems.

Have you thought about how you'd spend your time after retirement?

I would like to be a role model for my granddaughters. As a woman who broke family traditions to study and come to work, I have already shown the future generation what is possible. I want my granddaughters to learn from my experiences. I want to travel the world with them.

How do you measure yourself? Do you have quantitative or qualitative goals that you track and measure yourself against?

I have never measured myself consciously versus any goals, quantitative or qualitative. At the end of the day, if I can sleep peacefully, I consider the day well spent. That is all.

What are a couple of words your family would use to describe you?

Systematic and disciplined. They would also say that I balance the professional and personal front well.

What is the one piece of advice you'd give your children?

The same guiding principle that I have lived by is to help people through their circumstances, and if you cannot help, then do no harm.

How do you approach difficult conversations and conflicts? Could you share what has worked for you?

Being open and taking the emotions out helps me get through conflicts and difficult conversations for me. Also, I don't like to keep things unresolved and on the back burner. I think it is best to face the challenge, tackle it head-on, and do it quickly.

What was the last vocational or professional course you took, and did it help you?

I have continually educated myself and kept myself abreast of things in life. I was married off during graduation and then moved to the US with my husband. I did courses in the Community college there. After returning to India, I had two kids and continued studying. I finished my bachelor's and did my MBA from ICFAI with honours, and am now pursuing my Doctoral program with ISB. I think the degrees and courses helped instil confidence in me, and I feel that I am no less compared to other management professionals, entrepreneurs, etc.

Do you have a connection with your hometown/place of birth/community?

I grew up in several places in India and abroad, so I cannot point to one place. But I do have a strong sense of community and make efforts to keep my extended family and family connected. I wanted my children to understand that too, and today I am proud that we are all connected despite being in so many different parts of the world. The community is a support system, an intangible asset where a lot of giving and taking happens.

My family belongs to Vempa in the East Godavari district, and we visit the place whenever possible.

What is the best form of giving back to the society you have experienced and would advocate for others?

I founded this group called Women In Network with a few friends of mine about 15 years ago. Every Sunday, we go to urban slums and spend two to three hours with the children. We had seven centres, which have come down to three in recent years due to various reasons. Our mission is to ensure that the children continue their education at government schools, and sometimes we sponsor the ones who are keen on studying in private schools. We have seen them grow in front of our eyes, and today many of them are employed. We open up the world for these children in a situation where their parents cannot show them hope to aspire. Two of the kids have, in fact, taken up Kuchipudi dance seriously with danseuse Sandhya Raju.

I strongly believe that women should volunteer at all ages and stages in life. This is the way forward for uplifting those who are less fortunate.

What is the legacy you wish to leave behind?

Whatever good I've done should get multiplied by the people surrounding me. I don't need to be famous or well known. If people around me can build upon whatever I have done so far and make the lives of other people better, then that would be great. That would be the best legacy.

How do you define happiness? How often do you find yourself in this state?

Small things and intangibles give me happiness, and I like to dwell in them. I am not materially oriented. I have been blessed, and whatever has come into my network, I have embraced and welcomed. I would say that 90% of the time, I am very satisfied with what I have and what I have done in my life.

Any lesser-known facts about you that surprise people?

I love to dance, and I love music. Only the people very close to me know that I love to shake a leg.

What does spirituality mean to you, and how does it influence your approach to life?

I grew up in a religious family, and at a young age, I became very conscious of what blind faith is and how it can hurt. I saw discrimination on the basis of caste, creed, religion, etc. and did not like it. I feel being a kind human being is the most important. I do not believe in rituals; however, I am very tolerant. Live and let live is my policy. I voice my beliefs more now compared to when I was younger. I also believe that people can choose what makes them happy. As long as no discrimination or hurtful acts are done toward others, I am fine.

What role has education played in preparing you for the role you are now performing?

To be honest, education itself did not play a role in what I am doing in life today. However, when I came into the public domain and got involved in policy-making, administration and so on, I could recollect some of what I learned during my bachelor's degree. When I entered the public domain, I used to feel a bit undermined amongst peers who were all technically qualified and doing my MBA and CFA gave a big boost to my confidence. I wanted to prove that I am not here for a free ride and that my capability, intelligence and talent can be channelled. I could do that a lot more confidently after acquiring my degrees.

Do you believe in discipline and routines, or are you a spontaneous person?

I fully believe in discipline and routines. I am very organised and systematic. Discipline and consistency help you get where you want to at the end of the day. Spontaneity cannot define life, especially when there is a lot at stake and so much is riding on you. Dedicating and allocating time and doing things consistently is the way to get results.

Hyderabad to Cyberabad

The tech revolution that put Hyderabad on the world map

The License Raj phase

When the world of computers was opening up, India was in its License Raj phase, with the central government stifling the efforts of entrepreneurs by controlling too many aspects of the industry. The 1970s and 1980s saw the MRTP Act, industrial policy, nationalization of banks and insurance, as well as highly restrictive import policies and foreign currency regulations.

While the manufacture of equipment within the country was monitored and capped, the import of equipment like computers took months to get all the necessary approvals. Duties of more than 100%, sometimes even 300%, used to be charged on hardware imports. In the absence of a Department for Information Technology or Software Services at that time, the Department of Electronics (DoE) used to be in charge of computers. The processes, procedures and bureaucracy formed an unconducive environment for the growth of the new and innovative field of computers and software services.

Tata Consultancy Services was a pioneer in the field of computer services, having started in 1968. It was geographically located in the Bombay region. TCS is truly the first Indian company to go through the ordeals of obtaining licenses and permissions for mainframe computers and the first that also exported software services, a requirement from a foreign currency exchange reserve standpoint at that time. Eventually, two cities in South India shot to fame as IT hubs -Bangalore and Hyderabad.

The Texas Instruments Pilot at Bangalore ushers in a new era

A look at the evolution of the Information Technology industry in South India leads to Bangalore, which paved the way before Hyderabad became a hotspot for IT. Texas Instruments was the first big multinational company that came to India for a captive R&D unit. The number of engineering graduates, the bright students from the IITs and the number of students pursuing research through PhD programs were much higher than in the US. Texas Instrument's reasoning was clear–India had an unmatched talent pool at a low cost.

However, the regulatory challenges for setting up an R&D unit in India were many. The vice president of Texas Instruments met with the Government of India and said they would establish operations in Bangalore, subject to certain conditions such as single window clearance, ease of import license regulations, ease in approvals of customs and excise matters, etc. To enable this, the central government appointed a Committee of Secretaries, and the DoE was given administrative authority to provide all the licenses. This paved the way for the STPI scheme to be formed. The Committee of Secretaries also closely monitored the project and frequently met to review and take action on enabling operations of Texas Instruments at Bangalore under the STPI scheme. Some of the key requirements from a global communications standpoint were the availability of a data link and the use of a satellite station. A dedicated satellite station was provided by VSNL, a government undertaking later sold to the Tata group in 2008. A 64 kbps half circuit from India to Intelsat and onward to the US used to cost about INR 40 lakh per annum at the time. Through a lot of ups and downs, the government managed to co-operate and work together with Texas Instruments, and the pilot of a captive R&D unit was the first big success of the STPI scheme in India.

The STPI Phases I & II

Taking a step back, we look at the first STPI unit of India in Bangalore. Mr J.A. Chowdary, working in the Standards and QC division of the DoE, became a joint director and was moved to the software division in

DoE, reporting to Senior Director Mr SS Oberoi. The department had the primary responsibility of reviewing and processing applications. In the meantime, in the background was a Special Secretary to the Government of India and Founder Director of the National Informatics Centre, Dr N. Seshagiri, a visionary who pioneered the IT industry in India. He played a key role in India's first hardware and software policy. He is credited with bringing about STPI in India by formulating the entire scheme.

Mr Chowdary was appointed as the Director of STPI in Bangalore as its first employee. He was made responsible for ensuring that Texas Instruments had its operations running smoothly by supporting them from a technological, communication and approvals standpoint on behalf of the government. Mr N. Vittal, Secretary at the DoE, helped smooth out a lot of issues, mediating with the central government and, over the course of time, modifying the scheme to help business enterprises. The key advantages of establishing a business within the STPI were tax holidays, ease of import licenses, export duty and other regulatory processes. Seeing the success of Texas Instruments, PSI Data, Hewlett Packard, Digital and others followed to Bangalore.

The country made a note of the success of Texas Instruments and started taking a different and more open approach to encourage the IT/ITES industry. Infosys, HCL Technologies and other Indian companies wanted to also enjoy the benefits of STPI, but the data communication link costs were prohibitive for them. To reduce the link costs, Mr N. Vittal went to VSNL and sought to lower costs. When this wasn't feasible, he made a request for STPI to get a telecom license so that they could directly provide satellite links at affordable rates. Subsequently, microwave communications technology was used to provide satellite links at distances from the Electronics Park to other places in the city as well. The locational constraint was thus removed, and there were no labour constraints or inspections despite being a 'Software Park'. The availability of satellite links at a distance was a deal breaker for the Indian and multinational companies in terms of the cost of operating business, and it hastened the IT revolution. Import licenses were issued within a day. These factors contributed to getting big IT companies under the STPI scheme.

The Bangalore STPI, which was operating under the DoE for a long time, paved the way for the next few STPI centres at Noida, Bhubaneswar and Pune. Each STPI unit operated as a separate society until 1991 when they were all amalgamated under the Societies Act.

An STPI scheme—but no takers in Hyderabad

After two years of experience in Bangalore, Mr Chowdary took a transfer to start the STPI in Hyderabad in 1989 while continuing to be the Director for STPI Bangalore. From a makeshift office near ECIL, the STPI-Hyderabad established a formal office at the newly minted HUDA Maitrivanam building in Ameerpet on Dussehra day of 1990. With the persuasion of Chief Secretary Mr Natarajan, and a go-ahead from the then Chief Minister of Andhra Pradesh, Mr N. Janardhan Reddy, the idea to establish a technology park in Madhapur was firmed up. Mr Hari Narayan, Secretary, Industries, was a very proactive and progressive leader, and he understood the importance of the internet as an essential service to get companies to Hyderabad. With his help and the push from the state government, the STPI got 10 acres of land for setting up a technology park (of which Hitech City is a part), 1.5 acres behind the NCHRD building at Jubilee hills, and an interest-free loan of INR 1 crore. The satellite towers were positioned at Jubilee Hills to enable internet access to faraway locations such as Tarnaka. The success of this was a key turning point in the development of Hyderabad as an IT city.

The road to this development, however, was a rocky one. Under the STPI scheme, free internet was offered under the pilot scheme for six months, but it was difficult to persuade small or big companies to join the scheme. The Hyderabad companies at that time provided on-site consulting services, sending people abroad on projects. Questions commonly raised by multinationals that were invited to set up operations at Hyderabad were—Where is the talent pool? Are there any IITs? Are there any good buildings and infrastructure in the city? What about international clients? Is there a good international airport in Hyderabad? How about international schools?

With most of the answers being negative, no one was willing to bet on Hyderabad, and Bangalore, Chennai and Noida were given preference.

Intergraph India Ltd. was the only multinational company that had a good office in Hyderabad at that time. To try and attract companies to Hyderabad, Mr Chowdary used to take all potential visitors and showcased the HUDA Maitrivanam building and the Intergraph offices. Needless to say, it was not at all enough to convince them. Foreign countries boasted of much better buildings and infrastructure. While the internet availability problem was solved, other questions continued, and with no good critical senior talent, international airport facilities and schools, a journey or stay in Hyderabad was not attractive to many.

One day, Mr Azim Premji and Mr Ramakanth Desai came to the STPI office and met with Mr J.A.Chowdary. They were looking to open a new WIPRO development centre and were considering Hyderabad, with headquarters already being established in Bangalore. Deeming WIPRO as the perfect anchor company, the state government decided to allot them four acres out of the 10 acres given to STPI to set up a campus near Hitech City. At this time, the Cyber Towers offices hadn't opened yet. It was a major milestone to get one well-known company to build their office in the Hitech City area at that time. Thus, the Wipro building was one of the earliest occupants of the Hitech City area.

A CEO for the State, 'Cyber'babu Mr Chandrababu Naidu

The Chief Minister of Andhra Pradesh Naidu from 1995-1999 and 1999-2004 was Mr N. Chandrababu Naidu. He was known for being tech-savvy and technology-obsessed, earning him the name 'CEO of Andhra Pradesh'. He was determined to compete with Bangalore and make Hyderabad a major hub for IT and BPO companies.

In 1997, he toured South East Asia and was impressed by the developments in Singapore and Kuala Lumpur, particularly the Multimedia Super Corridor in KL. Mr Chowdary and Mr Randeep

Sudan, Special Secretary to Chief Minister, used to regularly meet with Mr Naidu to shape the IT industry policy and attract business to Hyderabad. During these meets, problems were discussed, and solutions were formulated. When the point was raised that international flights couldn't land at Hyderabad – the government immediately started work on extending the runway at Begumpet airport and initiated discussions on building a new international airport at Shamshabad. The next big challenge to address was the absence of a readily available and high-quality talent pool.

The Birth of IIIT

When the issue of manpower supply in Hyderabad came up, a brainstorming session was held and was attended by Mr J.A. Chowdary, STPI Director, Mr Ramalinga Raju, MD of Satyam Computers, Mr Bhalerao, Education Secretary of State, and a few others. They discussed how to build a talent pool in Hyderabad. It was concluded that IIT quality education with a focus on Information Technology was needed. Thus IIIT–International Institute of Information Technology, Hyderabad, was born.

A series of decisions were made to speed up the process and fulfil the objectives.

- To save time, an existing building and land were allotted that were originally meant for the district collectorate and magistrate offices and judge's quarters.
- To ensure a talent pool ready for the industry, an industry connect was established.
- To ensure diversity, a university would be created without any reservations. This was possible only if it was not a government university. Private funding was invited, and the university was set up as autonomous. IIIT was one of the early public-private partnership models in education.

The IIIT, established in 1998, has won several accolades over time, and many world-renowned centres of excellence are part of its portfolio. It has established various joint collaboration and co-innovation models with an industry outreach spanning significant national and multinational companies.

Very Important Visitors

The next big game changer was getting Microsoft to establish their first campus outside the United States in Hyderabad. Clearly, this didn't happen easily. In 1997, during his first visit to India, Hyderabad was not on Mr Bill Gates's itinerary. So with the help of Mr Frank G Wisner, Ambassador to India, Mr Naidu made an appointment to meet Mr Gates in New Delhi, where he was meeting with several Indian dignitaries. Mr Naidu, who was given a 10-minute slot, used a Microsoft Powerpoint presentation and talked for 30 minutes to Mr Bill Gates and did his best to sell Hyderabad as a potential site for Microsoft offices.

Soon after, the first site evaluation visit to Hyderabad by Microsoft teams was not successful. Mr Naidu, however, did not give up. He personally requested Mr Gates for Hyderabad to be given a second chance. On the second evaluation meet, he left no stone unturned. The teams worked hard to ensure that the best opportunities, incentives and infrastructure were provided. This saw success, and Microsoft announced they would establish their R&D centre in Hyderabad. Needless to say, this was another big feather in Hyderabad's cap, adding to the publicity of the city.

The first Microsoft office opened in 1998, led by Mr Srini Koppolu, with a few floors leased in Cyber Towers. The famous Leed-certified campus in Gachibowli was inaugurated on Microsoft's 10th anniversary in 2008 by the then Chief Minister Dr Y.S. Rajasekhara Reddy. Today, the Telangana government continues to be on very good terms with Microsoft, which is in talks to establish a massive data centre in Hyderabad in the coming years.

In 2000, when American President Bill Clinton was slated to visit India, Hyderabad was not on his agenda. To bring him to Hyderabad, the then Chief Minister, Mr Naidu, his team, and the STPI team decided overnight that an AmCham chapter should be started in Hyderabad.

The lobbying techniques of Mr Naidu were successful, and President Clinton visited the city. This event brought even more publicity and media mileage for Hyderabad.

President Clinton's favourable comments about the e-license and e-governance models in the state helped Hyderabad score many brownie points, and the city became a globally visible IT destination.

The formation of Cyberabad

In November 1998, the Cyber Towers or Hitech City building was inaugurated by late Prime Minister Atal Bihari Vajpayee and Chief Minister Mr Naidu. The STPI moved its offices from the HUDA Maitrivanam complex to this building.

Hyderabad Then and Now

Hitech city   Hitech city

During a visit to Malaysia in 1997, Mr Naidu and the STPI teams were impressed by the superb infrastructure of the multimedia super corridor with optical fibre cables and other impressive amenities. The need for building multiple buildings and offices in Hyderabad was imminent. When Malaysia, with limited tech manpower, was able to build a huge area, there should be so much more potential in a city like Hyderabad, felt Mr Randeep Sudan and Mr Chowdary. They requested Mr Naidu that the city needed many more buildings to call itself an IT hub. One building in Cybercity was not enough. The AP Industrial Infrastructure Corporation created a special subsidiary for the approval of buildings in the Madhapur zone. The area was identified and declared as the one to develop the new city, and the term 'Cyberabad' was coined soon after the Malaysia visit.

To bring more enterprises to Hyderabad, the government representatives and Mr Chowdary used to visit other cities, meet multinational companies, and make sales pitches about Hyderabad. On one such visit, Mr Chowdary of STPI, Ms Sheela Bhide, Mr Jayaprakash Narayan and Mr Neerabh Kumar, all IAS officers who discharged duties in various roles in the AP government, together went to Mumbai. They made individual presentations to BAAN, Citigroup, Oracle and others. During the visit, they showcased all the advantages of Hyderabad and put forth various incentives. BAAN

The Y2k crisis, Hyderabad's opportunity

Meanwhile, at the turn of the century, the world was brooding over the Y2K crisis. A slew of training centres came up in Ameerpet, teaching Mainframes, Cobol and Java technologies. In fact, so famous was the training hub in Ameerpet that there was a joke in  Silicon Valley that if one wants to know what the latest technologies are, then a visit to Ameerpet, Hyderabad will reveal what they are. Numerous technology companies in the city also took advantage of the requirement of these technologies by hiring and training their associates to solve the Y2K problems. Some also entered into BPO and KPO opportunities. Suddenly, Hyderabad started becoming a Y2K and BPO capital, with General Electric, Dell, and a few others setting up offices in Hyderabad. Thus, a world crisis became an immense opportunity for Hyderabad.

---

and Citigroup both agreed, and Hyderabad got its first official IT Park in the form of the 'Vanenburg IT Park', which used to be known as the 'BAAN building' for a long time.

Satyam, Wipro, TCS and Infosys started focusing on Y2K problem-solving. Several training institutes sprung up in Hyderabad. The Y2K wave in Hyderabad was followed by an ERP wave with BAAN, SAP and Oracle training and tools flourishing. The establishment of the

BAAN R&D unit in Hyderabad helped start a hub in the city. Initially, the BAAN ERP training was exclusively provided by STPI, Hyderabad, in collaboration with the BAAN R&D unit. This led to much international interest in Hyderabad, and companies entered into contracts and started getting other services such as software development, remote infrastructure management, etc. from Hyderabad.

Developers such as L&T, Raheja and DLF came and started constructing commercial space in the newly anointed Cyberabad area. Once the land and building infrastructure came up, attracting more companies became easier. The Indian School of Business campus came up in Gachibowli in 2001. International flights began operating, and international schools started operations in Hyderabad. Mr Naidu also used his skills to influence the Insurance Regulatory Development Authority to set up headquarters in Hyderabad. The US Consulate coming to Hyderabad is also to his credit. With the immense opportunity to digitize banking and the potential of fintech, banking and insurance, the financial district corridor was developed.

Phase 2 of the growth of the city thus saw the coming up of the Indian School of Business, Financial District and several office buildings, technology parks and commercial areas on the side of town that has come to be Cyberabad.

A note on chip design companies

During this growth phase, VLSI chip designs were predominantly in Bangalore, Pune, Delhi and Chennai, in that order. There was a huge struggle to get talent in Hyderabad. Mr J.A. Chowdary started Portal Player with collaborations from Silicon Valley, using bright talent from IIIT who trained in San Jose and Seattle. Portal Player designed the chip that powered Apple iPods and eventually got acquired by Nvidia Graphics. The establishment of Veda -VLSI design academy by Dasradha Ram Gude in Tarnaka was a big boon for VLSI design and the chip industry. Mr Gude's training academy trained people on VLSI and made the availability of local talent in the city easy. Softronics and other companies are associated with Veda, which solved the manpower issue for companies like Intel and other chip design companies.

The Satyam Saga

Once upon a time, Satyam was the prized jewel, Hyderabad's homegrown technology behemoth. Established by the visionary Byrraju Ramalinga Raju in 1987, Satyam Computers opened doors for thousands of Indian engineers. A vast campus at Bachupally included state-of-the-art training facilities and recruited fresh talent from top engineering campuses across the country. The client list boasted of leading multinational companies, including Microsoft.

Satyam made its way to become a listed company and eventually employed about 40,000 people. The company was listed on the NSE, NYSE and Euronext and was India's fourth biggest IT company, focused on the enterprise segment. Mr Ramalinga Raju shot to fame and, together with the leaders of Wipro, TCS and Infosys, were empanelled in several associations, chambers and networks of repute. Satyam Technology Centre and Satyam Computer Services were household names in (combined) Andhra Pradesh.

In January 2009, Mr Ramalinga Raju confessed to an accounting scam to the tune of INR 7,000 crore. It was a shocking scandal that rocked the corporate world and sent investors into a tizzy. The overall loss for investors has been estimated at INR 3,300 crores. The events have been chronicled in books such as The Satyam Saga, The Case that Shook India and The Double Life of Ramalinga Raju. After detailed investigations by the SEBI, 10 people, including Mr Raju, the auditors, the CFO and others of Satyam, were convicted of fraud in 2015, with several of them being sentenced to jail for seven years.

In 2013, after several hiccups and a multi-year process, Satyam was acquired and merged into Tech Mahindra. The company now operates as Mahindra Satyam and is the fifth largest technology company in the country.

DID YOU KNOW?

The HUDA Maitrivanam complex was the first successful incubator and accelerator for tech companies in the entire country. The tech companies, co-located with STPI, benefited from being early in the game. Mr J.A. Chowdary used to interact closely with them, helping by providing import licenses at their desk, in a short time and in an efficient manner.

The entire Information Technology training industry sprung around this area. Thus, the late 1990s and early 2000s were buzzing with computer technology training institutes in the Ameerpet area.

Software companies came together to start an association in this building, known as the Hyderabad Software Exporters Association (HYSEA), in 1993. Today, HYSEA has more than 300 registered members representing more than 90% of the IT industry in terms of revenue and headcount.

All the companies that started at the HUDA Maitrivanam complex either got listed on the US stock exchange or Indian stock exchange or got acquired by large listed companies in the US. This building is, in fact, India's first successful incubator and accelerator.

Some of the prominent companies that started their journey at the Maitrivanam complex are:

- Intelligroup Asia Pvt. Ltd. was the first US-listed company that came out of Hyderabad
- Sonic Wall -they built one of the first cyber security systems and got listed in the US in 1999
- Sriven Computer Solutions-got acquired by Metamor, which is now part of PSI Net.
- DataTree Systems Pvt. Ltd-They offered the first text-based BPO services in India and were acquired by First American Corporation.
- Infotech Enterprises, now Cyient-started with digital mapping technologies. It is one of the tech companies that has the largest offering in the engineering and technology space.
- Kernex Microsystems India Ltd. built Train Collision Avoidance Systems— and went on to get listed on the BSE.
- Crosscheck Technologies was working on chip-testability for semiconductor vendors; it was acquired by PolicyOne
- Smartsoft was acquired by Capital IQ Information Systems, a provider of financial information that became a part of Standard & Poor's McGraw Hill
- Pramathi Technologies, the first <u>middleware</u> product company, too came out of the extension of HUDA Maitrivanam at Aditya Enclave.

The Startup Scene-a journey over two decades

While the early 2000s witnessed several KPO, BPO, and VLSI design service startups, there was reluctance to start R&D units and innovative startups. Meanwhile, the early entrepreneurs, together with STPI, started building associations and networking groups. The Indus Entrepreneurs (TiE) Hyderabad was established. The Amcham Chapter was created. With the commencement of operations of the Indian School of Business (ISB) at Gachibowli, an industry-university connect called 'TiE-ISB Connect' was established. Initial business plan competitions conducted in Hyderabad yielded very poor results. At that time, the mindset of the city's people was not yet mature for VC funding and innovative thinking, which are essential for a startup ecosystem. There weren't a lot of risk takers in the city. Most people prefer to put their spare money into real estate investments. The early venture funds in the city were Venture East, which moved out and Hitwell Angel Fund, which closed down.

Both IIIT and ISB were asked to start incubators to get the culture of innovation and entrepreneurship going in the city. Educational institutions started flourishing in the meantime. In addition to IIIT and ISB, Hyderabad got a BITS Pilani campus, an IIT campus and NALSAR. Hyderabad for Innovation (H for I) was conceptualized by industry stalwarts and leaders of all these educational institutions. The schools started introducing a culture of innovation and entrepreneurship as elective courses. Mr.J.A. Chowdary (STPI), Mr Srini Raju (iLabs), Mr Srini Koppolu (Microsoft), Mr BVR Mohan Reddy (Cyient), Mr Ramesh Babu (Medwin), Prof P.J. Narayan, Director, IIIT Hyderabad, Prof. Rao, BITS Pilani Mr Ajit Rangnekar, Dean, ISB, Hyderabad, Prof Desai, Director, IIT Hyderabad, all came together for H4I. Some of these people started Hyderabad Angels with an aim to provide the angel funding round for the city's entrepreneurs and attract venture funds for further rounds.

During 2004-2009, the Government of Andhra Pradesh continued its efforts to bring global companies under the aegis of Chief

Minister Mr Y.S. Rajasekhara Reddy. Meanwhile, the Rajiv Gandhi International Airport was inaugurated in 2008 by Mrs Sonia Gandhi. Mr Y.S. Rajasekhara Reddy helped accelerate the Jawaharlal Nehru Outer Ring Road construction, an 8-lane highway about 158 km long. With connectivity by air and road tremendously improved, more Fortune 500 companies started coming to Hyderabad. Across different sectors, big multinational companies started establishing key operations or R&D units in Hyderabad.

In 2014, the State of Telangana was formed. Under the able leadership of the Chief Minister, Mr K. Chandrashekar Rao and the young and dynamic Minister of Municipal Administration and Urban Development, Industries & Commerce, and Information Technology, Mr K.T. Rama Rao, the culture of innovation and a strategic appeal to big companies to establish operations in Hyderabad and Telangana continues. The Telangana Hub, established in 2015, is a tech innovator and accelerator. Telangana is the first state with a wing especially focused on women entrepreneurs, the WE-Hub. In the last five years, the Telangana T-Hub has promoted talent and helped the funding scene in the city grow exponentially. Located in a 70,000-sqft. Office at the heart of the Hi-Tech city, T-Hub has enabled and helped over 1,800 startups since its inception. Most recently, the Parliamentary Standing Committee on Information Technology visited the T-Hub and was extremely impressed. Several other incubators and venture funds have come up in the city, and tech-enabled startups have seen success.

Mr K.T. Rama Rao had announced 2020 as the year of Artificial Intelligence (AI) for the state and recently released a report highlighting the achievements made during the year, despite the pandemic. Telangana AI's mission aims to position Hyderabad among the Top 25 global hubs in the world. A collaboration between the top technology schools of the city and leading technology multinationals saw a slew of events hosted throughout the year. Among other good news, Amazon Web Services announced plans to invest about $2.77 billion in Hyderabad and Microsoft, about $2 billion for data centres. Fintech has its own corridor in Hyderabad's Financial District. There are more than 200 fintech startups in Hyderabad.

Mettle

With the state government-aided schemes and support, as well as the entrepreneurial instincts of the locals, the availability of a very large and diverse talent pool and infrastructure, Hyderabad is poised to retain a prominent role in the tech world. It may even become the Silicon Valley of India.

Disclaimer

The views expressed in this book are the author's own. The facts are reported based on information gathered from secondary sources, and the author and publishers are not in any way liable for any errors.

Sources

Several online and offline research methods were employed in putting together this book. The sources primarily consist of websites and online articles, and papers put together and available publicly. The sources were verified when feasible

The facts are reported based on information gathered from secondary sources, and the editor and publishers are not in any way liable for any errors.

A list of some of the major data sources are:

Newspaper articles from The Hindu, The Businessline, Economic Times

Websites of featured companies:

Granules India Ltd.
LV Prasad Eye Institute
Rainbow Children's Medicare Ltd.
Dodla Dairy Ltd.
NCC Ltd.

Mettle

NCL Industries Ltd.
KNR Constructions Ltd.
Premier Explosives Ltd.
Elico Ltd.

Websites of educational institutions and organisations mentioned:

Biological E Ltd.
Center for Cellular and Molecular Biology (CCMB)
Genome Valley
National Institute of Pharmaceutical Education and Research (NIPER)
Venkateshwara Hatcheries Group
The International Crops Research Institute for the Semi-Arid Tropics (ICRISAT)
Defence Research and Development Organization (DRDO)
Telangana Hub (T-Hub) Website
Telangana Tourism website

Editor's Acknowledgements

A lot has gone into the making of the book. As I look back, publishing this book has been a journey unto itself. I express my heartfelt gratitude to everyone who made 'Mettle' happen.

Each of the accomplished interviewees gave me their time and sincere answers and helped me in my journey of telling their stories to inspire and motivate readers.

Jayesh Ranjan, IAS, Principal Secretary to Government of Telangana, Departments of I&C and ITE&C for writing the foreword for my book

P Sandeep and Viswanathan NS for helping me design the framework and prepare for the interviews through mock interviews and relevant feedback.

Subhajit Saha of the Telangana CII Chapter and my friend Raminder Singh Soin for helping me connect with individuals who have contributed to the book.

For the industry evolution, I thank the following individuals for their key perspectives

- K.Bhasker Reddy on the dairy industry
- J.A.Chowdary on the IT & ITES sector.
- Y.D.Murthy on the infrastructure construction and building materials industry
- Suresh Rayudu Chitturi on the poultry industry.

Mettle

Vinod Menon for pushing me to pursue my idea and being with me every step of the way.

Sekkizhar Balasubramaniam for believing in me and connecting me to several people crucial to getting this book together.

Friends and family for encouraging me in my journey with this book and participating in all the small victories along the way. Without you, I would have never made it!

www.ingramcontent.com/pod-product-compliance
Lightning Source LLC
Chambersburg PA
CBHW020907180526
45163CB00007B/2648